CONTINGENCIES AND OTHER ESSAYS

CECIL GRAY

CONTINGENCIES
AND
OTHER ESSAYS

ML
60
G795

GEOFFREY CUMBERLEGE

1947

OXFORD UNIVERSITY PRESS

LONDON   NEW YORK   TORONTO

OXFORD UNIVERSITY PRESS
AMEN HOUSE, E.C.4
London Edinburgh Glasgow New York
Toronto Melbourne Cape Town Bombay
Calcutta Madras
GEOFFREY CUMBERLEGE
PUBLISHER TO THE UNIVERSITY

PRINTED IN GREAT BRITAIN

Contents

Preface

THE FOLLOWING essays are selected from an output extending over a period of no less than twenty years, and it would consequently be strange if the writer's views had not undergone some modifications in the course of such a considerable lapse of time. Actually however, on re-reading them for the purposes of the present volume, I was at first agreeably surprised, and then slightly disconcerted, to find how little my fundamental beliefs and convictions had changed in the course of these many years—initially surprised at the consistency, and subsequently disconcerted by the plausible explanation of arrested mental development.

However that may be, I felt it better to leave unaltered any such minor discrepancies as might here and there exist between the opinions or points of view which I held in former days and those which I hold now. It may be true that second thoughts are better than first thoughts, but third thoughts are better still—and, incidentally, have generally more in common with the first than with the second. If I were to attempt to alter my former views and judgements in order to conform with those which I hold at the present time, I should probably find myself impelled, in the course of another few years, to change them again, and, as likely as not, back to those originally expressed. I think it best, therefore, to leave these essays untouched, in the hope that, whatever may be their shortcomings and imperfections, they reflect in their various ways facets of the truth. The whole truth, and nothing but the truth, does not lie within the capacity of any man.

The only exception is the biographical study of Carlo Gesualdo, Prince of Venosa, which was first published nearly twenty years ago as part of a volume written in collaboration with Philip Heseltine (' Peter Warlock '). The book has long been out of print and unobtainable. In view of the fact that the original documentary material on which the study was based—in the libraries, museums and archives of the city of Naples—has largely, if not completely, disappeared in the course of the recent hostilities, its re-publication, for the benefit of scholars and students of the period, seemed desirable. At the same time I was not satisfied with it as it originally stood, and consequently it has been subjected to considerable revision and re-writing.

Two of the essays, on Brahms and Liszt respectively, were contributed to *The Heritage of Music*, edited by Mr. Hubert J. Foss and published by the Oxford University Press. For the rest, thanks are due to the editors of *The Music Review*, *Music and Letters*, *The Musical Times*, *The Listener*, and *The English Review*, for permission to reprint contributions which originally appeared in these journals.

C. G.

LONDON,
1946

Contingencies

THOSE WHO lived through the years 1914–18 will remember that they were productive of a vast amount of active speculation concerning the probable and possible effects of the war upon art. While those with progressive sympathies rejoiced at the prospective crumbling of the bulwarks of effete tradition as a result of the upheaval, through which they would triumphantly float to power and influence, the representatives of reactionary tendencies were similarly pleased to think that the war would put an end to all that ' modern ' nonsense and would usher in a period characterized by a reversion to what they considered saner and more normal ideals. On the main issue both contending factions were fundamentally in agreement, namely, that everything was going to be quite different from what it had been in the years prior to 1914. Each of them, in fact, would have been more prepared to admit the likelihood of its own discomfiture and overthrow than the possibility that everything would go on in the same way as before.

Which, of course, is apparently what happened. After the temporary jolt and dislocation entailed by the conflict, life, and with it art, resumed much the same course as before, in all essentials. The academics went on being academic, and the revolutionaries revolutionary, as if nothing had happened; in no respect was there any visibly important change.

To-day there is once more a recrudescence of speculation concerning the effect of the present war upon art, and the probable changes it will bring about in the art of the future. It is natural that there should be, but while indulging in it we shall be wise to bear in mind the experience of the preceding generation, and the prosaic, negative outcome of all their wishful thinking—to use the hackneyed but inevitable phrase.

Even with this warning example before us, however, it is difficult —impossible, rather—to resist the conclusion that there is a fundamental difference between the two wars. The former one, apart from its gigantic scale, was not in essence very different from most of the other wars which have been waged since the beginning of history—a struggle between jealous rival nations and conflicting interests of a predominantly material and commercial order. Ingenious, but mostly ingenuous, propaganda on both sides was able to evolve all manner of ideological justifications for the conflict, but they only succeeded in convincing those who wished to be convinced, and in preaching to the converted. Democracy and the rights of the smaller nations, for example, sounded very well until one reflected that Czarist Russia was on the same side as the angel Democracies, and that Ireland was a small nation. The propaganda on the other side was too grotesque to be taken seriously by anyone.

The present war, on the other hand, is not primarily materialistic or commercial, but rather idealistic and ideological—a conflict between two opposed and irreconcilable ways of life. There is, indeed, a profound difference in feeling between the two wars which everyone who has had the misfortune to live under both must inevitably recognize. If the war of 1914–18 did not affect the arts to any appreciable extent, the reason is that it did not go deep enough. The present conflict, on the contrary, has its roots far down in the very soil from which art itself springs. On the former occasion the war, however immense in scale and tragic in human implications, was essentially external. It was possible for the artist, provided he survived physically, to escape from it into an ivory tower of his own construction, or into the recesses of his inner consciousness. To-day no such escape is possible. It is not merely that everyone is more immediately and directly involved, or that no ivory tower yet constructed can stand up to high-explosive bombs— it is more than that. It is no longer possible to take refuge within oneself, because even if we try to do so we find the conflict raging there as violently as in the outside world. In every artist to-day, in every sentient, pensive personality, the same tragic struggle is being waged; and even were one to travel to Peru or the Argentine one would take it with one. There is, in truth, no escape to-day, for any one, from the death pangs of the old world and the birth pangs of the new—for that is what is happening now, beyond any possibility of doubt.

The present war, in fact, is not just 1914–18 all over again, or

2

continued; everyone who thinks or feels knows deep down in himself that the old order, for better or for worse, has gone and will never return. Nothing is more remarkable than the tacit unanimity with which this is conceded. Not even the most crusted and hidebound Tory attempts to delude himself, or others, that there is the slightest chance of a restoration of the old world order, and this is as true in matters of art as in politics or anything else. One may even doubt whether anyone, in his heart of hearts, really wants it, for it is already dead, beyond recall. The recognition of the necessity for a ' new order ' is, in fact, by no means confined to the Axis Powers. The only points of divergence are, the nature of this new order, and who is to have the making of it. Its inevitability is nowhere seriously disputed.

The war itself even, is ultimately irrelevant—it is a symptom, not a cause. The impending dissolution of the old world, and the impending birth of the new, had been apparent to every thinking person long before the tragic conflict had begun. All it has done has been to precipitate, accelerate, and exteriorize, in the domain of international politics, an inevitable historical and spiritual process.

Events in the world of politics and action, generally speaking, are seldom anything but a coarse and crooked refraction of what has already taken place in the field of thought and art. In precisely the same way that the French Revolution took place in the writings of Voltaire, Rousseau, Diderot, d'Alembert and innumerable others, long before it found political realization; so the new order of the immediate future is clearly adumbrated by many thinkers, chief amongst them Nietzsche, Karl Marx and, before them, Hegel, who is the Janus-faced father of both Communism and Nazism by way of the Marxian dialectical materialism on the one hand, and the doctrine of the absolute totalitarian State on the other. They are, in fact, twin births. Their superficial hostility is that of brothers, springing from the fact that they understand each other only too well, and have so much in common. The greatest hatreds and antagonisms are those of affinities, of relations. No wars are more bitter than civil wars.

Nor are literature and philosophy the only channels through which new currents of thought and feeling first manifest themselves.

3

On the contrary, all the arts share to some extent in this prophetic, anticipatory, premonitory rôle. Verdi, for example, was the real creator of the Italian *Risorgimento*; neither Mazzini and the intellectuals who preceded him, nor the men of action, Cavour, Garibaldi, who followed him, could have succeeded if he had not lit the flame in every Italian heart by means of his music. Note, too, how the passing of the contemporary old order is symbolically anticipated in the ' dying fall ' which is such a familiar characteristic of the music of the last generation—the way in which the music at the end of a work ebbs away and fades into silence and nothingness—a procedure that has no parallel in the music of any other period. Debussy and Delius are in this respect the most characteristic exemplifications. See also in this connection the similar endings, in literature, of *Ulysses* and *Finnegan's Wake* of James Joyce, and T. S. Eliot's:

This is the way the world ends, not with a bang but a whimper.

All real wars and battles, the ones that really matter in the history of the world, first take place in the soul of man, and it is there that the issues are decided, not on battlefields or in political conferences. Nothing of importance is ever decided by force of arms—that is a vast delusion. As often as not, in history, the cause which ultimately triumphs is not the one which achieves the most superficially spectacular victories. The military successes of Napoleon, for example, outnumbered and outweighed his defeats, but he left France smaller and weaker than he found her. At the same time, the ideas of the Revolution, of which he was the instrument, spread all over Europe in spite of his ultimate military defeat.

In any case, military issues are generally decided by some completely fortuitous, accidental occurrence, of an essentially comic order. In no other form of human activity, except cards and horse-racing perhaps, does the element of pure chance play such a dominating rôle. To take Napoleon again, we are told by competent military historians that he only lost the battle of Waterloo owing to the fact that one of his commanders kept his troops marching backwards and forwards in wrong directions during the whole course of operations and only arrived on the field when it was too late and all was over. If he had got to the right place at the right time, Napoleon would in all probability have won the battle. But would it have made much difference in the long run? It is more than doubtful. The issues at stake had already been decided; the military decision was irrelevant.

Incidentally, this general's name was Grouchy, but it should have been Groucho, the most eminent of the Brothers Marx, of whom one is irresistibly reminded, especially in the battle sequence of *Duck Soup*. In the world of ideas, indeed, events may, and probably do, march with the inexorable logic and inevitability proclaimed by Karl Marx, but in the world of action they generally happen much more in accordance with the conceptions of the Marx Brothers. And with the best will in the world, it is impossible to take such comic turns as Hitler and Mussolini any more seriously than the Marx fraternity. They have even much in common—the same streak of sinister sadism, for example. The disappointment one experienced in seeing *The Great Dictator* of Charles Chaplin derived from the fact that the original was so much more richly comic than the caricature. Actually, the photographic sequence, which appeared in illustrated papers, of Hitler receiving the news of the French capitulation, was very much funnier than anything in the Chaplin film.

The truth is that statesmen and politicians are nearly always comic or second-rate figures, and it is only natural that they should be, for the very simple reason that no one would ever want to be a politician who could succeed at anything else. The desire to dominate others is in itself a sign of inferiority, shared by dictators and women. Politics are the last resort of failures, and it is no coincidence that Hitler and Mussolini began life as unsuccessful artists—painter and writer respectively—and that Goebbels and Ciano were both spectacularly unsuccessful dramatists before taking to politics. Even Napoleon himself, as a young man, began with literary ambitions, and Disraeli is another good example of a second-rate artist becoming an eminent statesman.

Mr. Churchill is another case in point. As a politician, he is, of course, in the first rank. He writes well, but not better than many hundreds of comparatively unknown writers at the present time, while as a painter he is not much, if at all, better than Hitler. (Incidentally, it is a remarkable coincidence that the war is being waged under the leadership of an undistinguished water-colour painter on one side, and an undistinguished oil-painter on the other. ' It makes you think ', in fact, as Mr. Nathaniel Gubbins' immortal Sweep would say.)

The truth would seem to be that the amount of talent required to make a successful statesman or politician will not get one very far in a purely intellectual or aesthetic activity; and, further, that second-rate and unsuccessful, disappointed artists, are, to-day at least, the commonest material out of which successful rulers of men are made.

It is, in fact, one of the most ominous signs of the times in which we live that artists who have failed almost invariably take to politics, as other men take to drink, in order to drown their sense of failure, and in order to realize in the sphere of action the conceptions—and the ambitions—they have failed to realize in art. The ranks of all political parties are filled with these aesthetic renegades.

Major artists, on the other hand, are almost always hopeless failures on the few occasions when they misguidedly meddle in practical politics, like Lamartine, or Chateaubriand, or Sheridan. They have too much talent for it, in fact, and only succeed in wasting their time and—or—in making egregious idiots of themselves.

The moral of all this is that art is art and politics are politics, and never the twain should be allowed to meet; that most of the trouble in the world to-day springs from the presence, at the head of political affairs, of inferior painters and writers and dramatists; and from the would-be artistic activities of persons who would be more fitly employed in affairs of State, or should be given posts as civil servants or schoolmasters. (A surprisingly large proportion of contemporary poets, incidentally, have begun as such, and should have continued as such—Auden and Co. for example.) One even feels, sometimes, that Sir Thomas Beecham, with all his gifts as a conductor, is essentially a politician *manqué*—that he would have made one of the greatest Prime Ministers England has ever had in her history if he had followed his natural bent.

6

It is difficult to say which is the worse of the two—the artist turned politician, or the politician turned artist. The result in either case is bad art, bad politics, and bad everything else. The confusion of the two activities poisons the world to-day, and this applies equally to all schools of political thought, whether Liberal or Conservative, Fascist or Communist, Nazi or Anarchist, and to all arts, whether literature or painting, sculpture or architecture— or music.

Mr. Calder Marshall, a characteristic exemplar of the amphibious type of artist-politician, has said in a recent essay in *The New Statesman* entitled 'The Pink Decade' dealing with his fellow writers of the 1930's, that he and his kind failed because, in spite of their (to him) laudable sentiments, in matters political, they did not take a sufficiently active part in carrying them into practice, and that 'the artists of the thirties who will interest posterity are the men of action, Malraux, Bates, Silone'.

Actually, Malraux is the only one of the trio with any claim to be considered an artist at all. Silone may be an able political propagandist who has written a very readable novel *Fontamara*, but it has no claim to be regarded as a great, or even a good, work of art. As for Bates, he is a complete mediocrity from every point of view, without the first idea of how to write. In the sphere of art, they are all insignificant, and they do not appear to be any more successful as men of action than they are as politicians. They are simply neither one thing nor the other.

At this point I seem to hear shrill bat-like squeaks and squeals from the Left Wing, which I must hasten to mute to the best of my poor abilities. The above strictures apply just as much to their opposite numbers in the political sphere—there is absolutely no difference between them in this respect. Ezra Pound, now 'on the spot' for broadcasting Fascist propaganda over the Italian air; Wyndham Lewis, one of the finest writers of our time and a draughtsman, if not a painter, of genius, now—at the time of writing—languishing in obscurity in Canada, largely as a result of having written pathetically naïve eulogies of Hitler in pre-war days; Roy Campbell, the greatest English poet of his generation, who fought on the side of Franco in the Spanish Civil War, thereby producing his feeblest volume of verse, *Flowering Rifle*—these are just as culpably futile in their political activities as their opponents of the Left Wing. The only difference between the two consists in the fact that Lewis and Campbell—I specifically except Ezra Pound—are finer artists than their opposites, but that is neither here nor there. No political significance should be attached to that coincidence—for it is nothing more. A plague on both their houses!

Among the scanty surviving fragments of Pythagoras is a repeated and emphatic injunction to his disciples to ' abstain from beans ', which puzzled learned commentators for centuries on account of its seeming frivolity, until it was realized that it was not, as at first supposed, the condition of physiological flatulence commonly engendered by eating the *faba vulgaris* that was the cause of the sage's censure, but the fact that in his time it was the custom to register votes in political elections by dropping beans into urns in accordance with one's convictions. In other words, Pythagoras' vehement injunction to initiates, ' Miserable wretches! keep your hands from beans! ' meant simply, ' Have nothing to do with politics! ' And to the modern artist one would utter the same warning.

This is not to say that the artist should be forbidden to entertain any political sentiments or convictions, but merely that he should take no active part in political activities. In so far as he is a human being he is bound to have some political views, but in so far as he is an artist he must not attempt to put them into practice. His rôle is that of spectator—not of participant. A spectator is not necessarily indifferent. On the contrary, his emotions can be just as violent as those of the active participant. One might even go so far as to say that they are more violent, but they are of a different order. The fact remains that the moment he leaves the auditorium and, carried away by his feelings, leaps upon the stage and begins to take an active part in the proceedings, he not merely interferes with the play, but also stultifies himself.

It is an accepted truism that the spectator sees more of the game than the player and is probably more emotionally moved by it, but it is the artist's sacred duty to keep his place as a spectator and not to interfere and take sides. Only by so refraining can he fulfil the lofty function for which he was intended in the scheme of things. The emotion attendant on the active participation in events is a very agreeable one, no doubt, and there is a great temptation to give way to it; but it is a grave dereliction of duty in one who aspires, however humbly, to the honourable appellation of artist; for in so far as he is an artist he is necessarily, inevitably, fatally, condemned to separation and detachment from his fellow men. It is his burden, his tragedy, if you like, but the penalty for the infringement of this natural law is artistic suicide. He ceases to be an artist, but without becoming anything else. The more eagerly he tries to overcome this primary condition of his being, the more completely he fails. When the artist of genuine creative talent seeks to play an active rôle in politics, it is as if the conductor of an orchestra were to lay down his bâton and to insist on taking the second bassoon part—and, incidentally, playing it very badly as a rule. A good example of this is to be found in the grotesque performance on the bassoon of M. Jules Romains, the distinguished French novelist and author of *Men of Good Will*, as recorded by himself in his recent preposterous book entitled *The Seven Mysteries of Europe*.

To this it might perhaps be objected that there are cases in history in which eminent creative artists have played a decisive rôle in political events—Byron, for example, and Gabriele d'Annunzio. The fact remains that the achievement of Greek independence would have come without the active intervention of Byron, that the prestige of his poetry was the determining factor in the success of the cause, and that in any case he would have been better engaged in carrying on with his *Don Juan*; while, as for d'Annunzio, he had ceased to be an artist of importance long before he took to politics. He is, indeed, the best example discoverable of what has been said above—that it is impossible to be an artist and a politician at the same time. You must make your choice, you cannot have it both ways. And the artist—and we mean by that the genuine artist—not the pseudo-artist or aesthete—who deliberately chooses to sacrifice his art for the sake of political action is guilty of a crime, the sin against the Holy Ghost of whom he is the mouthpiece, the chosen instrument.

Thought precedes action, art anticipates politics, as we have already had occasion to observe. To renounce art in favour of politics is to abandon the substance for the shadow. Politics are only a second-hand, crude, belated and imperfect realization, in the material sphere, of ideas and conceptions already full realized in the domain of art and pure thought. The function and the duty of the artist is, not to attempt the wholly superfluous task of bringing to fruition in the field of present political action the values of yesterday's thinkers and artists (superfluous, because it will be and can be better accomplished by others and without his assistance)—but rather to play a part in the inception and formation of the ideas, values, concepts which are destined to be the guiding principles of to-morrow. That is the rôle of the artist; to be a pioneer, not a camp-follower; a prophet, not a politician. The artist who refrains from meddling in politics, and ' keeps his hands from beans ', is not, as so many callow, half-baked intellectuals to-day suppose, an escapist. It is he who is, on the contrary, in touch with reality; it is they who are the escapists.

In this connexion should be cited a highly apposite passage from Mr. Cyril Connolly's *Enemies of Promise*:

Often a writer who is escaping from his own talent, from the hound of heaven, will run into what appears to be reality and, like a fox bolting into a farm kitchen, will seek sanctuary in group activities from the pursuers outside. And after a time the hounds will be called off, the pursuit weaken, a signal that the Muses no longer wish to avail themselves of his potentialities. Thus, among the hardest workers in political parties will be found, like Rimbaud at Harar, those whom the God has forsaken.

Arthur Rimbaud, who at an early age suddenly gave up writing and became a merchant in Abyssinia, is the most conspicuous and celebrated example in history of an artist of talent, of genius even, who turned his back on his art. For this act of apostasy he has always been venerated and held up as a noble example by all artists who have similarly become disillusioned and uncertain of themselves; the idea being that in so doing he renounced Illusion for Reality, the Ivory Tower for the Market Place, Art in favour of Life (all with very large capitals). This is, of course, nothing but an inverted ninety-ish aestheticism, and only incompletely inverted at that. The fact that Rimbaud became an Abyssinian trader in ivory and frankincense casts a tawdry glamour, in the large watery sheeps' eyes of our aesthetes, over the sordid fact that a heaven-born (or rather hell-born) talent surrendered his birthright in order to become a kind of grocer with the frankly avowed ambition of making money. One doubts whether they would become so ecstatically admirative if he had become an *épicier* in Menilmontant—yet that is what, in essence, and robbed of its romantic trappings, he did.

The plain unvarnished truth about Arthur Rimbaud is that he could not face himself and his problems, and his artistic difficulties, and that he ran away from them, and sought refuge in the existence of a typical French *petit bourgeois* from the terrible and terrifying realities which confronted him. It is a familiar type, particularly in France. Montparnasse used to be full of them—young artists who eventually became *sages* and gave up their work in favour of a safe commercial career. There is no mystery about it, and there should be no halo. Rimbaud's sole desire in his later years was to make a little money and marry, settle down, and live respectably, like a good French *bourgeois*.

A very reasonable and understandable ambition, and one which every artist must experience at some time or other in his career when the dark night of the soul descends upon him and he doubts himself and his art and everything else—and the greater the artist the oftener and the more intensely does he experience it. Art is the hardest and most exacting vocation on earth, and one can well understand and sympathize with any man who modestly finds it too much for him, or himself unequal to it, and decides he had better give it up and try something else. All one objects to is the attempt to make a virtue out of his deficiency—which, to do him justice, Rimbaud never attempted to do—to represent himself as superior to the mere artist, and to have discovered a Higher Reality than mere art. Even worse is the Sidney Carton attitude so many examples of the type assume, in pretending to sacrifice the selfish sweets and joys of the artistic life for the rigours and hardships of politics and reality in the service of humanity. ' It is a far, far better thing that I do ', etc. This is truly insufferable. He who does so is not a hero but a coward, a traitor, a renegade. He is given by

God, or whatever inscrutable power it is that created life and living things, the rarest and most precious of all gifts, and he throws it away. He has no right to do so, even, for it is not his to dispose of. It belongs to the whole of mankind; he is only a custodian with a sacred trust. The artist is no more free to do what he likes than a king is. He has not even the latter's right to abdicate, for there is no one to take his place, no one else who can do exactly what he can do.

The plain, prosaic truth is that the artist's function is to create works of art, and that this is a whole-time job, and one that demands everything a man has to give, and more. No one can hope to be a good artist who has any time or energy to spare for politics, which is also a whole-time job; and there can be no hope for art in the new world which is to come unless and until the fatal confusion which has grown up between art and politics in recent times is broken down.

Both governments and artists have been equally to blame for this —Communist and Fascist attempts to dictate to the artist what he must think and say and do, and even the way in which he has to do it, and on the other hand attempts on his part to interfere in matters which do not or should not concern him. If there is anything worse than State interference in matters of art, it is artists interfering in affairs of State. The artist must be free to express himself in his work as he wishes—this right must be inviolable—but in return for this privilege, he should refrain from making a nuisance of himself. His political convictions, like his religion and his sexual life, are his own affair, as long as they remain private, but if he insists on putting them into practice in the market place he has only himself to blame for the consequences. It is a form of indecent exposure. In the lamentable controversy which took place two or three years ago over the signatories to the so-called 'People's Convention', both parties were equally to blame; the B.B.C. for attempting to dictate to artists the kind of political views they were to be allowed to hold, and the artists for trying to interfere in matters which did not concern them, as artists—for their signatures were requested and given *in their capacity of artists*, be it remembered and not of mere private individuals, Tom, Dick, Harry, to which no one could have taken exception, but to which no one would have paid any attention.

The matter is of primary importance, because if artists do not learn prudence in this respect, there is a danger that in this country in the future they may find themselves in the same unpleasant position as their comrades in totalitarian States. And that is simply the death of art.

Verdi remains the perfect example of the attitude which the artist should endeavour to maintain with regard to politics. It need hardly be said that no one was ever further from being an art-for-art's-sake aesthete, dwelling apart in an ivory tower, or indifferent to the problems which beset humanity. On the contrary, he was a passionate patriot and, as already observed, probably did more to bring about the *Risorgimento* than any other single individual. But he resolutely refused to take any part in politics as such. He was made a senator of the new kingdom of Italy, but against his will, and took no active part in parliamentary proceedings. If, swept away by facile emotion in his youth, he had given up his work in order to become a member of the *Carbonari*, not only would the world have been poorer, through the loss of his music, but also the very political cause he had so much at heart.

The moral of all this is, that if an artist's work is animated by passionate political convictions, he can disseminate and propagate them, but only through his work; that if he wishes to wield political power and influence he can do so, but only by writing good books or music or painting good pictures—not by making speeches, serving on political committees, or signing manifestoes.

The writer of the present essay takes the opportunity here afforded to state that he has no political convictions whatever, save for an occasional leaning towards Jacobitism (as distinct from Jacobinism—who was Jacob anyway?) on the one hand and Nihilism on the other; and since neither of these creeds can be said to be practical politics, it follows that he has no political axe to grind. The only axe he has to grind is that of art, and from its grinding the sparks will now begin to fly.

Let us turn to the consideration of the form of art, and more particularly that of music—the art with which we are here primarily concerned—which is likely to prevail in the days to come, after the war is ended.

Many people, of course, believe that there will be no art at all, worth speaking of: that art, being the delicate flower and fragile blossom of civilization, must inevitably be the first thing to go, and artists the first people to suffer.

The present writer does not share this view. He believes, on the contrary, that art, so far from being a frail and fragile blossom, is an extraordinarily strong and tenacious growth, and artists remarkably tough and resilient people. They have to be, in order to survive at all, like adventurers in other walks of life who have to live from hand to mouth, from day to day, quite literally by their wits, and taking no thought for the morrow. As for art, it is no doubt perfectly true that much, if not most of it produced by the order of civilization which is now dying, was an exotic hot-house plant, and that it will wither away if it has not already done so, but it is not true of art as a whole. The form of art which is only a kind of spiritual luxury will certainly go, like all other luxuries, for the time being. It is inevitable. Life is going to be very much harder in future, and for a long time to come, and art also will be harder, simpler, plainer. The caviare and *pâté de foie gras*, the champagne and oysters, the brandy and cigars of art, as well as of life, of the soul as well as of the body, are going, if not already gone, and a very sad business it is in many ways. No wishful thinking here. No one could be more blissfully and unrepentantly addicted to such joys in both the spiritual and physical worlds than the present writer, but one must face the facts, however disagreeable.

But just as food is a bodily necessity in some shape or form, as well as a possible luxury, so art is a spiritual necessity as well as a luxury. Mankind cannot live without it. The specious view of Hegel and others to the effect that art belongs merely to an early phase of human development, and that it has already outlived its prime and is virtually a moribund anachronism to-day, must be emphatically rejected. Among the earliest records we possess of the existence of the human race are works of art—and very good ones too—such as the cave-paintings of Altamira and the Dordogne, and they will probably be among the last records of the human race. As for music, D. H. Lawrence has said somewhere that ' In the beginning was not the word, but a chirrup ', a lark singing in the dawn of time; and in the great night of the universe, when the sun has entered upon an irrevocable decline, and the last stars are being gradually extinguished, one by one, like guttering candles, the final expression of sentient life will probably be the song of the nightingale.

There is even a considerable amount of good scientific evidence to support the view that the world itself, the entire created universe, is itself a work of art, that God is an artist, and that on no other basis or supposition can the scheme of things become intelligible. At any rate, all attempts to explain or justify it according to the tenets of religion or philosophy or ethics or morality have so far failed, and are likely to continue to do so; but once accept it as a magnificent (and frequently preposterous) spectacle, and all difficulties vanish away.

However that may be, art has always existed in the world from the earliest times up to the present day, and it is therefore reasonable to suppose that it will continue to do so. In any case it will take more than a war, however catastrophic, to eradicate an instinct which is as natural to man as eating, drinking and copulation. It is as fundamental as these—no less.

Many who would agree with this contention in general, nevertheless regard the immediate future of artistic activities with deep misgiving, on account of the acute financial stringency which, in their view, must inevitably ensue upon the conclusion of hostilities, in consequence of which there will be no money available for such superfluous luxuries as art.

This argument is, of course, only a corollary to the foregoing one, and the answer to it, so far as it has not already been made, is that, firstly, if we can find fourteen million pounds a day for the war (this is the figure at the time of writing—it is probably much larger now) there should be no difficulty in finding the few hundreds a day which should be more than enough to establish artistic activities on a more secure basis in this country than they have ever yet enjoyed. If the desire, the demand, the need are there, the money will be forthcoming.

But in any case the argument is rooted in a fallacy. The chief trouble with art, in the days before the war, consisted in the fact, not that too little money was spent on it, but too much. That it was spent in the wrong way, dissipated in wrong directions and objectives, may be true, but does not alter the fact. A few suggestive observations from an article in *The Observer* by C. A. Lejeune, the film critic, aptly illustrate this point:

The nations that suffered most from the (last) war, Germany and France, began within a couple of years to build up the finest cinema they had ever known. Out of material poverty came richness of ideas. Out of devastation came renaissance. . . . The early and middle 20's saw the Golden Age of the German cinema. Cut off from the outside world, with little money to spend, the Germans fell back on their own rich store of invention and legend . . . the best films have always come from pinched nations shut down on their own resources.

It does not, of course, necessarily follow that what is true of the cinema is true of the fine arts; but, nevertheless, I believe it is fundamentally true that vast sums of money lavished on artistic enterprises, or paid to artists, do more harm than good, both to art and to the artist. Too much money is just as bad as too little, and probably worse. Too little starves the body, but too much kills the soul.

Contrary to the generally accepted belief, great art does not often go hand in hand with an exceptionally high degree of material ease and prosperity, whether we are speaking of civilizations, races, nations, classes, or individuals. One could even go so far as to say that peoples living in a comparatively primitive state of culture have a more direct, instinctive, and vital appreciation of art than those which have enjoyed luxury, ease and opulence. At the Porta Capuana in Naples, for example, one used to hear professional reciters reeling off whole cantos of Dante, Ariosto and Tasso, to an enraptured and enthusiastic audience of illiterate peasants and workers, while at cafés near by one would see the members of the upper or middle classes—the so-called educated classes—immersed in their daily newspapers.

16

Similarly in Florence, when the simple hard-working men and women of the city and environs enjoy a brief spell of leisure, you will see them in their hundreds thronging the galleries of the Pitti and Uffizi, but you will find few of their ' betters ' there—they prefer a different kind of picture house. Again, the opera houses of Italy are filled with large and enthusiastic audiences made up chiefly of the common people; the upper strata of society for the most part prefer jazz, and dancing in smart hotels. In Italy an artist, as such, is an object of respect and even veneration to the masses; the aristocracy and middle classes prefer to pay homage to the heroes of the football field or the motor race-track.

The secret of the strength of Italian art, and particularly music, in the past, is largely to be found in this immediate contact and understanding that exists between the artist and the people. It is also the source of its weakness, of course; great works such as *Otello* and *Falstaff* have never been really successful in Italy—they appeal only to the few. But, taken all in all, the advantages outweigh the defects.

In France precisely the contrary conditions obtain. The average Frenchman and Frenchwoman of the working classes are probably more completely indifferent to any form of fine art, and to music in particular, than any other people in the world. On the other hand, there is probably in France a larger proportion of members of the upper classes of society capable of taking an intelligent interest in the higher manifestations of art than anywhere else, and in the subtleties and refinements of style, especially where literature is concerned; and the existence of this large, select, and discriminating audience has, of course, exercised a considerable influence on artists in that country.

This also has its great merits and advantages, and also its defects. One might say that if the chief virtue of Italian art, in general, consists in the fact that it is almost a physical necessity, a kind of food, like bread or wine, fruit or vegetables, French art tends rather to be an embellishment or enhancement of living, like flowers. The difference between them can perhaps be best symbolized by comparing the signification we attached to the words meaning ' taste ' in the two languages—*gusto* and *goût*. They are at root the

17

same word, and ostensibly possess the same meaning, but their overtones and implications are very different.

If in Italy art is essentially popular and proletarian in its appeal,
and in France primarily aristocratic, in Germany art has chiefly
been directed at and appreciated by the middle classes; and while
the appeal of Italian music is largely sensual, of French music intellectual, that of German music is chiefly emotional.

All three traditions, as already suggested, have their drawbacks
and deficiencies. Italian art is often coarse, crude, blatant; French
art is often dry, mannered and emasculate; German art is often
sloppy, sentimental and effusive; but these faults are in the balance
greatly outweighed by the positive advantage that the artist has, in
each of these countries, in possessing a solid background of tradition,
and a potential audience willing to pay attention to him.

In this country nothing of the kind exists. Neither upper nor
lower nor middle class as a whole, or even in part, cares for any
form of art, and perhaps, least of all for music. The artist has no
cultural background, no national tradition, no public, save for a few
individuals scattered here and there in upper, lower and middle
classes indiscriminately, and possessing no lowest common denom-
inator or highest common factor. Otherwise the only support
music has enjoyed in these islands in modern times has been of the
kind generally accorded to religion, and due to a belief that music
is in some vague, unspecified way, good for the soul, like going to
church on Sunday; and all the more salutary for being a bit boring
—for if it were too enjoyable it would not be so improving, or up-
lifting, or edifying. Hence, incidentally, the enormous vogue of
Brahms in this country, so much greater than in the land of
his birth. Brahms has almost become a British composer by
naturalization.

The inevitable consequence of these conditions has been a complete lack in this country of that element of tradition and continuity
which one finds elsewhere. Indeed, one might almost say that this
is itself a definite national characteristic—that our great figures have
always tended to appear as isolated individuals rather than as members of a school, or participants in a universally recognized and
appreciated tradition—uniqueness, separateness, isolation, in fact,

might paradoxically enough be regarded as the English tradition, and characteristic of the national genius in all walks of life. We rather pride ourselves on this tendency. We speak, for example, of 'our one and only Shakespeare', and most of the great figures in our literature are similarly unique and singular. So in painting—Hogarth, Blake, Turner, Constable, are all detached, isolated individuals. So in music, with our one and only Purcell, and his one and only opera, *Dido and Aeneas*. Even in political history, it is interesting to note, one finds the same curious propensity for producing a solitary specimen in a category—for example, our one and only Holy Roman Emperor, Richard of Cornwall, and our one and only Pope, Nicholas Breakespeare, who took the title of Hadrian IV ('our one and only Breakespeare', as Joyce has it in *Finnegan's Wake*)—and other examples could be multiplied indefinitely.

This tradition also has its advantages and its defects, but here the defects outweigh the advantages. It does not matter so much in literature which, in any case, is the one and only art which has always enjoyed a certain measure of public support in this country. All that is necessary in order to write is a pen or pencil and a writing pad, and there is never much difficulty in finding a publisher, or for a painter to find one or two intelligent patrons. So far as these arts are concerned our traditional individualism works out fairly well in practice, with, of course, a few regrettable casualties *en route*. But if anyone in this country should be so ill advised or regrettably constituted as to wish to erect cathedrals or carve blocks of marble, or write symphonies or operas, even a comfortable private income will prove inadequate to the problems involved in the material realization of his conceptions. In these arts the lack of any organized public demand is fatal, especially in music. Even the most enthusiastic and richly endowed composer after twenty or more years of creative activity under such circumstances begins to ask himself whether it is worth while to go on writing masterpieces for his own personal pleasure, which are for the most part destined to remain unrealized, unpublished, unperformed, in a drawer of his writing desk. After all, a work of art is essentially a collaboration between creator and recipient; all the more so in music in which

19

the work does not, strictly speaking, exist on paper, but only in the act of performance. Elgar, in comparison with most of his colleagues a spectacularly successful composer, once observed that it was impossible for any English composer to reach the age of sixty (I quote from memory, but the exact words are immaterial) without becoming completely cynical and disillusioned.

It is an exceedingly depressing state of affairs; all the more so because there is no reason to believe that there is less potential musical talent in this country than in any other, or that intrinsically the British public is less musical than any other public. As I have pointed out in *Predicaments*, history shows that there is no such thing as a specifically musical or unmusical nation—that the most musical at certain periods becomes the least so at others, and *vice versa*; that in the sixteenth century England was probably the most musical race in Europe, and Germany the least; that there is no reason why it should not be so again, and that there is every reason to suppose that it will.

But before any such reversal or transformation can take place a change must come about, or be brought about, in the attitude of the public to art generally, and to music in particular in this country. It is impossible for an art such as music to thrive, or even to be in a moderately healthy condition, which has virtually no audience apart from a sprinkling of aesthetes and 'highbrows', forming a kind of layer of sugar icing on the stodgy plum-cake of British philistinism. A composer cannot live—and by living one means something much more than mere physical and financial subsistence —through contact with this thin veneer or upper crust of intelligent appreciation alone. Without a substratum of popular appeal no art can be healthy or vital.

The recognition of the truth of this contention has brought about in recent years the development of an activity known as 'musical appreciation', which aims at fostering a love of music among the populace by means of broadcast lectures, evening classes, elementary handbooks and textbooks, educational gramophone records, and so forth; by teaching music, in a word, in very much the same way as one would teach any other subject in the educational curriculum. The belief is even entertained that it is possible to inculcate an understanding of the most ' advanced ' music, provided the student works long enough and hard enough at it, as he would at the differential calculus, or quadratic equations.

With all respect to the many well-meaning, devoted and enthusiastic members of this faculty of musical appreciation, one cannot help feeling that their activities are based upon a complete fallacy, namely that it is possible for aesthetic sensibility to be imparted or acquired, or even developed, by any such methods of spiritual jerks or intellectual Sandow exercisers. The foundation of all aesthetic enjoyment lies in the direct, unfettered, unreflecting response to a sensual, emotional, imaginative experience, and no amount of lectures or evening classes can take its place, nor can they enhance it. The musical appreciationists make the mistake of starting at the wrong end, from what should be the final stage of aesthetic appreciation—the intellectual and analytical—and working backwards in the hope of arriving at the first—pure enjoyment. It cannot be done. It is like attempting to produce the flower or blossom without first cultivating the plant.

A direct, emotional response even to a comparatively unworthy object will take one further on the way to genuine aesthetic understanding than any number of courses of musical appreciation. In other words, it is better to enjoy wholeheartedly, say, a march of Sousa or a waltz of Lehar, than to be able to make a thematic analysis of a Beethoven sonata and yet remain unmoved by it, or less moved by it than by Sousa and Lehar. *Bonum est in quod tendit appetitus*—the good is that towards which the appetite tends—thus spake St. Thomas Aquinas. These words should be printed in letters of gold over the portico of every concert hall and opera house in the world. They are the foundation stone of all true aesthetic experience.[1]

The musical appreciation movement no doubt has its uses. It may be of value to those who already react emotionally and instinctively and directly, and serve to deepen their pleasure by adding to it a certain intellectual element, but it is very doubtful. This aspect of musical art, the intellectual and analytical, is best

[1] Compare this with the utterance of the great modern English painter, Walter Sickert: ' Pleasure, and pleasure alone, is the proper purpose of art '.

left to the active practitioner and withheld from the passive recipient. It is valuable and even necessary to the composer, the critic, the executant, but the ordinary listener is better without it. In art as in everything else, a little learning is a dangerous thing, and often does more harm than good.

Again, while it is certainly undeniable that the activities of the musical appreciationists have resulted in a greatly increased superficial interest in music on the part of a large section of the general public which had previously never paid any attention to it, there is an inverse side to the picture which usually escapes attention.

A little mass observation and Gallup surveyance in public places and public houses, carried out by the present writer, tends to confirm the belief that for every convert enlisted in the ranks of music-lovers by the appreciationists, at least two more are antagonized, through being led to imagine that music is a thing one has to be ' educated up to ' before one can hope to enjoy it, instead of, as it should be, pleasure, first and foremost, and all the time; to which, later perhaps, other more intellectual, but less important and vital experiences may be added. Any suggestion of uplift or education in connection with pleasure inevitably tends to put off more people than it attracts, however unjust and wrong-headed and pig-headed this may be. We all know from personal experience that when children are told that rice or sago pudding or spinach is ' good for them ' they automatically distrust and avoid these things, and the average adult is in no way different when it comes to art. The faintest suggestion, the slightest hint of improving his mind or cultivating his soul makes him as restive as a wild horse; he whinnies, paws the ground, and makes off as hard as he can go.

One should aim rather at making it clear that art is primarily pleasure, like eating, drinking, or copulation, only more lasting and intense, and with none of the disadvantages that attach to over-indulgence in these otherwise delectable activities. It would even be better if one could teach people to regard indulgence in art as a vice rather than as a virtue. One would like to see them sneak furtively into concert halls as if they were public houses, in order to have a quick one before closing time—anything would be better than this atmosphere of education, uplift, improvement. These

22

latter elements are present in great art, of course, but they are incidental; we should not mention them, any more than one should mention to the child the powder that is concealed in the spoonful of jam. If you emphasize the good that the powder is going to do, you will only succeed in making him suspicious, even when you offer him a spoonful of jam and nothing else. And actually, of course, that is what art essentially is—a spoonful of jam. One should try to induce people to regard music as children regard jam. It is only the beginning, admittedly, but it is a necessary beginning, the only possible beginning. *Bonum est in quod tendit appetitus.*

In this important connexion a little anecdote will be instructive, the truth of which can be vouched for, since it came to us at first hand. There was once a small boy, a member of what used to be called 'the upper middle class', who was brought up, like most members of that class, to have a deep-rooted distrust and contempt of art, and especially 'classical' music. He possessed a gramophone, and his taste was deplorable, his records consisting exclusively of vulgar comic songs, popular sentimental ballads, cheap waltzes, and so forth. One day he bought by chance a record entitled *Carmen March*, under the blissful delusion that the title referred to the carmen for whom one used to see signs outside cafés inviting them to a 'good pull up'—a curious title for a march, admittedly, but this did not occur to him. It was, of course, an arrangement of various themes from the opera of that name. On playing it, he found that he enjoyed it far more than all his other records. On discovering his ridiculous mistake in the matter of the title he was emboldened to progress further on the path thus accidentally opened up to him and, to cut a long story short, this small boy—now middle-aged, alas, enjoys his Bartók, Berg, and Schönberg with the best of them.

This is an extreme case, no doubt, but it is typical of what is going on all the time, as a result of the deeply ingrained distrust and suspicion and dislike of any kind of educational or moral uplift in the British public in connexion with art. The boy would not have bought that record if he had known it was a piece of 'classical' music, as the saying is. This prejudice is not as strong to-day, perhaps, as it used to be, but it is still much stronger than many

23

people realize; and musical appreciation, with its educational approach, undoubtedly tends to strengthen this antagonism to art in the mind of the ordinary man in the street, to a far greater extent than it develops an already existent love of it in a certain smaller section of the community.

In the higher strata of society this national prejudice against all art, and especially music, has its roots largely in the attitude of mind and code of moral and ethical values formerly inculcated at our public schools and universities; what Messrs. Robert Graves and Alan Hodge in *The Long Week End* describe as ' the Spartan virtues of modesty, reticence, courage, generosity, loyalty, personal cleanliness, and general decency. . . . With the Spartan virtues went the Spartan prejudice against all things artistic, eccentric, abstract, poetic, studious, foreign, or feminine '.

This is a perfectly accurate diagnosis. The personification of the qualities enumerated above is the absolute antithesis of everything that is implied in the word ' art '. The English Gentleman, who is the final perfected product of our methods of education and psychological training, is the complete Philistine—the Philistine in the mind of God, to speak platonically. He is, of course, the very type of the man of action, the administrator, the civil servant, the statesman, and very successful the ideal has been in achieving the purpose for which it was intended.

It is, in fact, no part of our intention here to decry the ideal of the English Gentleman. The Bloomsbury intellectuals and the aesthetes who are accustomed to sneer at it are quite wrong to do so. ' Modesty, reticence, endurance, courage, generosity, loyalty ' and the rest of it—these are all very fine qualities indeed, and only a fool would sneer at them. The best type of English Gentleman is in many ways the salt of the earth, but, unfortunately, it is an ideal which is, inevitably and necessarily, achieved at the expense of all the qualities—virtues and vices—which go to the making of great art and great artists. Every human ideal demands the sacrifice, the extirpation of all qualities which conflict with it, and the English Gentleman, like the Confucian Sage and the Medieval Saint, is the perfected product of an age-long tradition and a life-long discipline which, however admirable in many ways, are bound of their nature to be rigidly exclusive. In short, to be a gentleman is a fine ideal, and one that is difficult of achievement. It requires enormous self-discipline, self-sacrifice, and a genuine nobility of character. To be a perfect gentleman is in a very real sense to achieve a work of art, but it is a form of art that excludes all others.

Let us look once more at the catalogue of virtues personified in the ideal of the English Gentleman, and apply them to the artist as we know him. The artist is not modest, or reticent; if he seems to be, it is only a pose, or a mask. More often than not he is a physical coward, mean, disloyal, and by no means devoted to personal cleanliness and general decency. In fact, the greater the artist, the less he exemplifies these admirable virtues enumerated above, and the more he exemplifies them, the less great an artist he is likely to be.

The artist is not a gentleman, in short, and it is customary in this country to bewail the fact, and to express amazement at what is naïvely supposed to be an inexplicable duality—a kind of Jekyll and Hyde business. The commonest criticism of Wagner, for example, is that he was a great artist, but a cad—as if he could be anything else. All artists are cads; it is impossible to be at the same time a great artist and an English Gentleman, just as it is impossible to be a great artist and a politician. (It need hardly be added that it is equally impossible to be an English Gentleman and a successful politician.) Choose which you will, but do not try to achieve both —it cannot be done. You will only fail at both. This was the tragedy of Elgar, born of his environment. He tried to be a great artist and a great gentleman, but he just failed to become either one or the other. To quote once more from Mr. Cyril Connolly's *Enemies of Promise*:

It is no exaggeration to say that every English writer since Byron has been hamstrung by respectability, and been prevented by snobbery and moral cowardice from attaining his full dimensions. It is this blight of insular gentility that accounts for the difference between Dickens, Thackeray, Arnold, Tennyson, Pater—and Tolstoi, Flaubert, Rimbaud, Baudelaire, Gide; it is the difference between being a good fellow and growing up,

and it is this blight of insular gentility that chiefly accounts for the difference between Parry, Elgar and Vaughan Williams—and Strauss, Debussy and Stravinsky.

Music, incidentally, is the art which in its essence, more than any other, is most in opposition to the ideal of the English Gentleman, and the musician is the most complete embodiment of all the qualities which are most repugnant to the public school and university tradition—'artistic, abstract, poetic, studious, feminine and foreign'—especially the two latter. Music, in fact, in orthodox English eyes, has been regarded as essentially an occupation for foreigners, and a recreation for women.

As a natural and automatic reaction against the cult of the English public-school-tie gentleman, we find the equally English phenomenon of the aesthete or intellectual, embodying, deliberately and self-consciously, all the qualities and defects which stand at the opposite pole to those enumerated above by Messrs. Graves and Hodge. He is the reverse of the coin, that is all; the product of a reaction against environment. The Philistine and Aesthete are at bottom one and the same, brothers under their skins. They accept the same values: the one positively, and the other negatively by reacting against them and mechanically inverting them.

It is difficult to say which is worse, from the point of view of art —the Philistine or the Aesthete. There is not much to choose between them. One might say that their chief difference consists in the fact that whereas the former likes the wrong things in the right way, the latter likes the right things in the wrong way. On the whole, one prefers the honest Philistine, if only on purely human and social grounds. The aesthete is almost invariably detestable, quite apart from his almost invariably homosexual propensities—which brings us to one of the most difficult yet important problems we are called upon to consider in these pages. Naturally, we shall not be able to do more than touch on the fringe of a vast and complex subject.

In the seventies and eighties of last century, largely as the result of the activities of Ruskin, Morris, Rossetti, Swinburne, Pater, and others, it almost seemed for a moment as if England, after a period of eclipse, might once more become a civilized country in which art might hold an honoured position as in former days. Then there

26

appeared upon the scene a talented Irish mountebank named Oscar Fingal O'Flaherty Wills Wilde, who succeeded in turning this promising artistic renaissance into an instrument for his own aggrandizement and notoriety. The art-movement became identified with Wilde, in the public mind, and was consequently involved in his ignominious fate.

The trial and conviction of Wilde were, in fact, a major disaster to the cause of art in this country, the importance of which cannot be exaggerated, and the effects of which have persisted up to the present time. In the public mind the name of Wilde became synonymous with the title of artist, and the title of artist with the practice of homosexuality. Even to-day, in this country, to be an artist is to be *a priori* sexually suspect in the eyes of the man in the street. Art and paederasty are indissolubly associated in his mind.

The trouble is that—Wilde apart—it is so often justified. The innocent reader would no doubt be surprised to learn how many of the most eminent and respected figures in the world of art to-day are known to have leanings in this direction, to put it mildly. The laws of libel, naturally, forbid individual specification.

The problem is a difficult one. The fact is, and has to be faced, that homosexuality is nearly always indicative of an advanced level of intelligence and artistic sensibility. The explanation of this disconcerting but incontrovertible phenomenon is probably to be found in the fact, that, while most normal males pass through a brief homosexual period during puberty or adolescence, they quickly emerge from it, whereas the specific homosexual remains at that stage; and this arrested sexual development, in accordance with the rules of the law of compensation, leads to an accelerated and intensified development of other faculties. This would account for the majority of such cases, but they are very seldom, if ever, creative artists of any stature or significance, belonging rather to the category of aesthetes—persons of sensibility and understanding, receptive rather than productive.

It is a very different matter when we come to consider the homosexual element which indisputably exists in some of the greatest masters, such as Shakespeare or Michael Angelo. The greater an artist is, the more he includes, the wider his range of feeling and

27

sympathy and susceptibility; in consequence of which his all-embracing circumference will inevitably contain, together with everything else, a certain streak of homosexuality. But that is not to say that Shakespeare or Michael Angelo was homosexual in the ordinary sense of the word, as defined above. Their whole mental outlook was not coloured by it, and determined by it throughout, as in the case of these others. They just happened to be homosexual as well as everything else—they included it, they took it in their stride, as it were.

A streak of homosexuality, in fact, and even a big fat slice of it, is probably present in every great artist, every outstandingly intelligent person; but it is only when it exceeds fifty per cent that we can legitimately call him homosexual.

Actually there is probably no such thing as a hundred per cent male, or female, for that matter. Even those specimens of the human race who are as much as ninety per cent male or female are generally intolerable, and exceedingly stupid and insensitive. Homosexuality, indeed, appears to be a kind of leaven mitigating the monstrosity of the absolute male and the absolute female. It is probably even true to say that the pleasantest and most civilized and intelligent members of the human race are essentially hermaphroditic, possessing the characteristics of both sexes in almost equal proportions. It is only when the foreign element, so to speak, preponderates, that the trouble starts. For while a certain proportion of homosexuality is not merely desirable, but essential in an artist, as indicated above, it is an unmitigated disaster when it amounts to an overplus. After all, sexual relationships are among the most important things in life, and are the source of all great art, however sublimated—perhaps most of all when sublimated. If this root is twisted and distorted, if this source is turned back on itself, the result must inevitably be an unnatural growth.

No fifty or more per cent homosexual can ever be a great artist. It will always and inevitably come out in his work in the form of a lack of balance or proportion, a false perspective. It is customary on the part of those who share homosexual propensities to refer to themselves and each other as being ' queer ', and the expression is a singularly happy and accurate one. Extreme and even excessive sensibility to some things goes together with complete anaesthesia to others; the balance is destroyed, and values are inverted.

A good example of this is to be found in Marcel Proust. Any discerning reader of *A la Recherche du Temps Perdu* must inevitably experience an uneasy sense of something unnatural and unconvincing in the loves of the hero (Proust himself, of course) and Albertine. It does not ring true; with all its intensity and power there is something odd about it, which is explained by the simple fact that Albertine in actual life was not a woman at all, but a young man. Proust, for reasons of his own, has tried to transfer or transcribe homosexual love into terms of normal heterosexual love, and it simply does not work, because the two things are entirely different—they belong to separate worlds, and have nothing in common.

A simple analogy may help to make this important point clearer. To us who live on the north side of the Equator the concepts of spring, Christmas, the north wind, the south wind, and so forth, have definite connotations, but for those who live on the other side, say in Argentina, the words convey precisely the contrary. The north wind is the balmy zephyr for them, the south wind is a cold blast from the Antarctic icefields, Christmas is tropically hot, spring is deciduous, and so on. The Argentine poet, then, who wishes to address himself to the understanding and sensibility of the European reader can only do so by mechanically transposing and inverting his imagery, which cannot be done without a hollow inner falsity, a kind of spiritual discord. And so it is with homosexuals; they speak a different language by nature, and when they seek to speak the language of normality we at once perceive there is something wrong—their utterance is unconvincing.

Particularly is this true of music which is, of course, the art with which we are chiefly concerned. It is a remarkable fact that this art which, paradoxically, is the one which in the eyes of the average Englishman, is the most effeminately suspect of them all should be the one to which the creative contribution of women and homosexuals is the smallest. In the whole history of music there is not a single outstanding female composer, and up to the present time only one male homosexual of eminence, namely Tchaikovsky.

29

From the creative point of view, in fact, music is, of all the arts, the most uncompromisingly masculine and virile.

How is this to be explained? Quite simply. As I have sought to show in my *Survey of Contemporary Music* and *The History of Music* —and I have yet to encounter a convincing denial or refutation of the thesis there set forth—music is the romantic art *par excellence* —the art in which the romantic values are most completely and perfectly expressed. (Do not expect here a definition of the romantic element in art. It would require a disproportionate amount of space, and in any case I have already attempted to provide one in the opening and closing chapters respectively of the two books above mentioned, to which readers are referred for fuller discussion and development. It is enough for the moment to say that although romanticism may be difficult to define, we all know what it connotes and implies.) And at the very centre of the circle around which the romantic values are described, in whatever age or clime you may find it—for it is universal and perennial, ever-recurring throughout time and space—one finds the cult of the adoration of woman in some form or other. In short the Christian, Medieval, Romantic values—they are all in essence the same thing—revolve around the idealization and idolization of woman, as exemplified in the cult of the Virgin, in the love of the troubadour Jaufre Rudel for the Princess of Tripoli (whom he had never seen), in the mystic passion of Dante for Beatrice, of Petrarch for Laura, in the conceptions of the *Ewig-Weibliche* of Goethe, the *idée fixe* of Berlioz, and the various Salvation Army *redemptrices* of Wagner.

I am far from wishing to suggest that all or even any of these manifestations of gyneolatry are necessarily admirable or desirable. On the contrary, it is probable that the feministic bias of modern western democracy, which is largely a consequence of these concepts, is wholly deplorable. But that is neither here nor there. We are only concerned at the present moment with a specific aesthetic issue, which is best summed up in the following inescapable syllogism; (*a*) music is the romantic art *par excellence*; (*b*) the romantic element in art, wherever we find it, immutably revolves around some manifestation or other of the worship of the feminine principle; (*c*) the musician, as such, is inevitably and ineluctably a lover of womanhood. It therefore necessarily follows that no homosexual, except perhaps a Lesbian, can possibly be a great composer. The truth of this generalization needs no further confirmation than that which is afforded by historic fact, namely that, as already observed, one can only find one possible exception to the rule in the history of music, and even this one is by no means of the first rank. Moreover, it requires no particular degree of insight to note that this tendency is written large over all Tchaikovsky's work. It betrays itself especially in his inveterate propensity for lapsing into mincing waltzes, and in the fact that his best work lies in the field of the ballet. He is indeed the ideal composer of ballet music—there is no better—but he is little else. Even his symphonies are for the most part merely ballets in disguise, and when Massine transformed his Fifth Symphony into a ballet one felt that it was being re-created in the medium to which it properly belonged—which one certainly could not say of the lamentable travesties perpetrated by Massine upon the Fourth Symphony of Brahms or the *Symphonie Fantastique* of Berlioz.

Ballet, in fact, is the homosexual art-form *par excellence*, and if the numerous homosexual composers at work in this country at the present time would take a word of kindly advice, they would confine their energies to the cultivation of this form, for it is the only one in which they can ever hope to succeed.

In view of what has been said above, it is no mere coincidence, but only what one would naturally expect, that one should find the most complete and perfect example of the homosexual in art to be that provided by the person and activities of the famous Russian impresario, Serge Diaghilev and his ballet, and in the enormous influence it has exerted—particularly, and significantly so, in this country. Despite the very considerable artistic merits of his productions and his undoubted flair for selecting the finest contemporary talents to serve his aesthetic purposes, one need have no hesitation now in saying that the influence which Diaghilev and his organization have had on art in this country has been wholly disastrous—firstly, in its direct influence on creative art; secondly, by confirming in the mind of the British public their already deeply ingrained belief in the fundamental relationship between art and homosexuality. We found ourselves back, in fact, in the ' naughty nineties ', with Oscar and Aubrey and the old Yellow Book all over again. The psychological atmosphere was identically the same. Homosexual art—in so far as it exists—never progresses, never develops, it will be noticed; it is always the same throughout the ages. And at performances of the Russian Ballet the character of the audience was frequently such as to render one's presence in the midst of it—if one happened to be comparatively normal—so acutely distasteful that one preferred to stay away altogether, missing thereby, no doubt, many otherwise enjoyable artistic experiences.

To-day in this country the ballet cult seems stronger than ever. It was practically the only form of artistic activity which, so far from having been halted by the war, had a positively new accession of strength. While the pre-war stream of concerts, plays, and operas, dwindled, during the first years of the war, into a mere trickle, new ballet companies came into existence every few weeks, and attracted large, uncritically enthusiastic, and fatuously hysterical audiences, which still continue.

There are, of course, other psychological reasons for the ballet vogue at the present time besides its appeal to homosexuals. The cult of the dance is invariably in evidence during the period of the decline and decay of a civilization, and in times of war, famine, and pestilence. The jazz-cult is, on a lower aesthetic level, another symptom of the same historical and hysterical conditions. Whatever the future of art may be after the war, we can at least be fairly sure that it will not take the form of a continuation of this *danse macabre*, this St. Vitus dance, which belongs to the world of yesterday, and is only the galvanic twitching of a corpse—like a chicken which runs around in circles after its head has been chopped off.

Incidentally it should be made clear that in all that has been said above concerning homosexuality there is no suggestion of puritanism or any implication of moral disapproval attached to it—one's objections lie solely on artistic and aesthetic grounds. Those who have these tastes are at perfect liberty, so far as we are concerned, to indulge them ' to the top of their bent ', as Henry James would say, and we sincerely wish them all the fun they can get out of it. All one asks is that they should refrain from attempting to practise the arts creatively, and music in particular, which is the most exclusively and uncompromisingly masculine of them all; and secondly, that they should not be placed in a position of influence or responsibility, not only because everything they do is coloured by their peculiar predilections, as is natural and inevitable, but also because of the subtle, pervasive system of freemasonry which they practise on each other's behalf. In this respect, indeed, they constitute a formidable menace in every artistic sphere in which they are active.

Of all forms of freemasonry, in fact, that of the freemasons is the mildest and most innocuous. Next in order of comparative harmlessness is that practised by the Scots, then that of the university and public school fraternity, then that of the Jews; but last and most powerful of all is that exerted by the homosexuals. From being a persecuted minority, like the Jews, they have gradually established themselves in a dominating position in much the same way. In the theatre to-day, as any actor or producer will tell you, it is notoriously difficult to succeed unless one enjoys their favour and influence. In music the same situation, if hardly as yet in such an acute stage, is nevertheless rapidly developing in the same direction.

On the other hand, homosexuals, precisely because of their creative incapacity, probably constitute the most sensitive and intelligent section of the artistic community in the passive and receptive sense, and the world of art would be very much the poorer without their sympathetic understanding and discriminating patronage of deserving artistic enterprises of every kind. The fact remains that they are by nature fundamentally parasitic—neither wholly creative nor wholly receptive, neither completely artists nor completely spectators, but partaking of both without ever quite becoming either one or the other—intermediate, in fact, in this as in other things.

Another species of morbid growth on the body of art generally— by no means confined to this country, as is largely the homosexual aesthetic type—is to be found in that infinite multitude to which Mr. Jacob Epstein refers in his recent autobiography *Let there be Sculpture*, of ' log-rollers, schemers, sharks, opportunists, profiteers ' etc. who, in his experience, infest the world of sculpture and

33

painting. Mr. Epstein is greatly mistaken if he supposes that this phenomenon is confined to the world of sculpture and painting; it is just as much in evidence in the world of music, if not more so, indeed. In the same way that the fairest countries in the world seem to be those which give rise to the largest number of minor drawbacks and discomforts and inconveniences—the beggars, the hotel-keepers, the mosquitoes, and other insects—so the noblest realms of the spirit seem to furnish the most favourable breeding ground for parasites and pests of every kind. During the first months of the war they all scuttled away into obscurity. It was good to be free of them, to breathe the pure, antiseptic, if sterile, air of the desert, to be alone with oneself in the wilderness. But since then they have returned, in even greater force than ever before. This is due to several causes. Firstly, as a result of the strict rationing of almost all commodities, and the consequent restriction of expenditure on them, the world of art has enjoyed a vast if largely artificial boom as an outlet of superfluous financial resources, in which music has naturally shared. Secondly, the native variety of Mr. Epstein's ' log-rollers, schemers, sharks, opportunists and profiteers ' has been formidably reinforced by an enormous influx of Central European refugees, largely of Jewish extraction, compared to whom, in technical virtuosity, our home-product is as a tallow candle to a thousand kilowatt arc-lamp. The consequence has been that, between the two varieties of thugs, the native and the foreign, the fair art of Apollo and Euterpe has become the happy hunting-ground of a rout of commercial speculators and profiteers. Music has become a black market, a ' racket '. The position, indeed, is precisely parallel to that which obtained in Prohibition days, in Chicago, under the rival gangs of Al Capone and Bugs Moran. The only difference consists in the fact that our rival musical gangsters have not yet taken to bumping each other off with sawn-off shotguns. One would welcome the salutary consequences of such a war of extermination, but, unfortunately, unlike their Chicago colleagues, our musical gangsters are much too clever for that. The only way in which to get rid of them—which must be done—is to diminish, if not to eliminate altogether, the financial inducements which alone attract this ignoble pullulation of the lower forms of life around the temple of the arts. In order to get rid of tapeworm, it is instructive to note, the only cure is to starve oneself, while seated on a chamber-pot filled with warm milk. After some days of this agonizing and Spartan regime the intruding parasite reluctantly decides to change its quarters, which it does through the highly appropriate orifice. The bowl of warm milk, after the war, will, of course, be America.

To a great extent this condition will operate automatically. In this country after the war there will not be the same amount of money to be made out of art as there was before, and that will be all to the good in more ways than one. As we have already said earlier in this essay, the chief trouble with art before the war was, not that there was too little money spent on it, and made out of it, but too much. That its distribution was unequal and unjust, as in every other walk of life, is true, but the fact remains that its reduction is a necessary condition to artistic health. The fantastically bloated salaries paid to eminent *virtuosi*, whether singers, players or conductors, the inflated performing-right fees earned by certain composers, and worst of all, parasitic ' arrangements ' of other people's ideas—all this must go.

This is not to subscribe to the outmoded romantic notion that it is good for an artist to starve in a garret—that hunger is a necessary condition for the production of masterpieces. No great achievement in art has ever been accomplished on an empty stomach— feats of saintliness, perhaps, but that is a very different thing. Nothing devitalizes the mind more than hunger, and while this is perhaps a necessary condition of saintliness—which demands a hollow vacancy to be filled by the breath of Godhead—it is at the opposite pole to art which demands that one should be well fed. Art, like nature, abhors a vacuum. But if there is a greater deterrent to artistic achievement than hunger, misery, poverty, it is ease, wealth, prosperity. We praise, and rightly, the man who triumphs over all obstacles and adversities; but equal, if not greater, praise is due to him who triumphs over all advantages, who keeps his soul intact in the face of recognition, fame, success, wealth. One can certainly think of many examples of the former, but very few of the latter, in modern times. It is more than probable, for example,

35

that his immense success was largely responsible for the spectacular decline of Richard Strauss, and he is typical of what seems to happen sooner or later to all contemporary artists who achieve fame and prosperity.

If both poverty and riches are antagonistic to art, what, it may be asked, is the solution to the problem? The ideal would probably be for artists to have a small independent income, like Manet or Cézanne; enough to keep them without financial worries and pre-occupations, but not enough for a life of ease and self-indulgence. Few artists, however, have enjoyed this condition, and in future there will be even fewer—if indeed, any private incomes are left after the war. Similarly, the solution afforded by the rich and enlightened patron of former times is not likely to survive in future.

The answer is to be found in the medieval institution of the ' corrody ', as it was called, in accordance with which a monastery would provide food, lodging, clothing, and all other necessities to scholars and artists, and would take their work in return. Under such conditions, free from the ceaseless preoccupation of earning a living, and at the same time protected against the equally soul-destroying effects of too great prosperity, it was found that artists did their best work.

Already, incidentally, a very similar principle is to be found in operation in Soviet Russia. Unfortunately, however, it is there vitiated by the obligation laid upon the artist of producing an ideo-logically orthodox kind of work, and also of comporting himself in strict conformity with the Communist code of morality. In this connexion see the sad fate of the composer Mossolov, as recorded in Kurt London's book on the arts in Soviet Russia: ' his life was full of women and alcohol, which was considered unsuitable for a young Soviet artist—he was dropped '. (There is an ominous sound in the last three words, as of a stone falling down a deep well.) That, of course, is where the Soviet system is bound to fail, for women and alcohol are a necessity to most artists, and should be amply provided for in our ideal corrody. Domesticity and art, on the other hand, do not run well in harness. Apart from Bach it is difficult to think of a great artist who has also succeeded in being a good family man. It is one of the many things for which we rightly venerate him, but it is not a model for lesser men to imitate. As we have already had occasion to observe in connexion with politics and the ideal of the English Gentleman, art and domesticity are both whole-time jobs, and he who attempts both must sooner or later make up his mind which of the two he is going to sacrifice, the alternative being to fail at both. Family life, then, would be not perhaps forbidden, but gently discouraged, in our ideal corrody.

Joking apart, however, some such system of State subsidy for the artist must come about in order to take the place of the rapidly vanishing, if not already extinct type of the patron, or Maecenas. Together with this ideal of a modest, comfortable sufficiency for the artist, and freedom from material cares, in place of the old alternative of excessive opulence on the one hand and indigence on the other, will go a similar change in the quality of art itself, and in the public response to it. No longer must art be a luxury for the few, and non-existent for the many except in a debased form. The soul-starved masses of the old order, like the body-starved masses, were a disgrace to our so-called civilization. Art must once more become for all what it originally was, a spiritual necessity.

Luxury, luxuriousness, opulence, these are the primary and essential characteristics of the art of the period which is over, of what for convenience we call the democratic, plutocratic order. The music of Richard Strauss, for example, is of a piece with the *Hotel Splendide*, champagne, caviare, oysters and *paté de fois gras* of the Edwardian era. The same applies to most of his contemporaries and immediate successors, such as Mahler, the early Schönberg of the *Gurrelieder*, and countless other examples. The characteristic vice of overscoring is significant—it is the gesture of the *nouveau riche*, the millionaire, the self-made man of art. The more money it cost, that was the test of excellence.

The art of the succeeding phase of the period, best typified by Stravinsky, is of a more subtle order, but remains essentially the same at bottom. His is the luxury of the cocktail bar and chromium-plated steel furniture; rather uncomfortable but *chic* and elegant, discomfort *de luxe* in place of comfort *de luxe*—but always *de luxe*. This kind of art has its parallel in fashionable slimming cures, the voluntary self-starvation of the rich, Miss Greta Garbo's diet of

37

carrot juice, the self-imposed martyrdom of winter sports in Switzerland or Scandinavia, with its accompaniment of broken limbs, and enduring the agony of peeling skin on torrid Mediterranean beaches at the height of summer, in order to achieve the fashionable beige tint. But perhaps the best symbolic embodiment of the spirit of the age was to be found in Gourdjieff's institution at Fontainebleau, where millionaires, duchesses and others would pay the Master fabulous sums in return for the privilege of scrubbing floors, breaking stones, and weeding the garden. Austerity *de luxe*, in fact, and the keynote of it all is ostentation, display, vulgarity—above all, vulgarity.

The art of every period has its qualities and its defects. Classical art, in decline or decay, tends towards aridity, desiccation, anaemia. Romantic art in decline and decay runs to fat, becomes vulgar. And never since the days of the decline and fall of the Roman Empire, when we find exactly the same thing (see Petronius, who, however, distilled an exquisite essence from its corruption, as scent is distilled from the secretions of the civet cat), has life and with it art, been vulgar in the way in which it is vulgar to-day—or, rather, was yesterday. It is the supreme, the unforgivable vice of the art of the past century, the age of middle-class civilization, of the dominance of the *bourgeoisie*. Even the finest artists of the age, in their weaker moments, lapse into vulgarity. Nothing, for example, could be more blatantly vulgar than Keats at his worst. Almost the only great nineteenth-century artist who is completely free from it is Berlioz. In his weaker moments he may be pompous, or coarse, or vacuous, but he is never vulgar; he oscillates between the aristocratic and the plebeian. He is never middle-class in either his strength or his weakness, and this is the chief reason why his art has as yet never been properly appreciated. He does not belong to his period.

For the rest, practically all are tainted by it, even those who are well aware of it, and react most violently against it. No one, for example, has diagnosed the disease more accurately and eloquently than Mr. Aldous Huxley, or satirized it so pungently; but nothing could be more vulgar than much of his own fiction. And the root cause of this unescapable vulgarity of our pre-war civilization is to be found in the worship of money, of riches, of material success and prosperity.

Well, all that has gone, or is going, and vulgarity will pass with it. There is no more certain antidote to vulgarity than suffering. Suffering ennobles, and this decadent vulgarity of the old world is being burnt out of us in the fierce furnace through which we are passing, and from which we shall inevitably emerge purified and refined.

After the most artificial and unreal period in history, we of to-day have been experiencing reality as no other people have before, to the same extent, in the form of the daily confrontation of death by all. There is no escape from it, rich and poor alike face the same conditions. At the beginning of the essay, it will be remembered, we put forward the thesis that art is reality in its purest and most essential form, and that art is most vital in a state of society which is in touch with the realities of human experience. It is consequently reasonable to assume that as a result of the ordeal through which we are passing there will eventually spring a reawakening of a genuine desire for art on the part of ordinary men and women, and a re-birth and revitalization of art itself. It is in this belief that the present essay is written.

It need hardly be said, I hasten to add, that one does not expect a kind of apocalyptic millennium of art—that the entire population of our cities and countryside are about to fill our concert-halls to overflowing in order to listen to the masterpieces of Bach, Beethoven and Mozart. The public for good art has always been a minority, and always will be. All we wish to suggest is that the minority will be a larger one than it was before.

To some, no doubt, even this will appear excessively optimistic. Mr. George Orwell, for example, in his brilliant little pamphlet *The Lion and the Unicorn*, says that

the place to look for the germs of the future England is in the light industry areas and along the arterial roads. In Slough, Dagenham, Barnet, Letchworth, Hayes—and, indeed, on the outskirts of great towns—the old pattern is gradually changing into something new. It is rather a restless, cultureless life, centring round tinned food, *Picture Post*, the radio, and the internal combustion engine. It is a civilization in which children

39

grow up with an intimate knowledge of magnetoes and in complete ignorance of the Bible. To that civilization belong the people who are most at home and most definitely of the modern world, the technicians, and the highly paid skilled workers, the airmen and their mechanics, the radio experts, film producers, popular journalists and industrial chemists.

One cannot help suspecting Mr. Orwell here of a certain streak of masochism, for he is an intelligent man and a highly gifted writer; at any rate he can certainly be acquitted of the charge of wishful thinking, for it is not a world that anyone possessed of artistic sensibility, as he is, can contemplate without a shudder. If the post-war world were, indeed, to be such as Mr. Orwell has depicted in the foregoing quotation, then, of course, there would be no hope, no future, for art whatsoever—there is no place for it in such a world. But Mr. Orwell, we are convinced, is wrong. The world he depicts with such devastating and depressing accuracy is a picture of the world as it was before the war, or, more accurately perhaps, as it would have become in due course if the war had not happened. In which case, however much we may deplore the war as human beings, as artists we can only welcome it as a blessing in disguise (very well disguised, admittedly), if it saves us from such a melancholy future as this suburban, Wellsian, brave new world— a fate worse than death. Mr. Orwell, in fact, seems to think that the post-war world will be like the pre-war world, only more so; we believe in a complete change, a transvaluation of values.

Already this belief would seem to be justified, and Mr. Orwell confuted—so far as music is concerned, though I believe that the worlds of literature and art tell the same story—namely, that after the period of complete stagnation which lasted from the beginning of the war to the end of the *blitz*, a wave of interest in, and enthusiasm for, the arts has been initiated and has reached a height and a pitch unprecedented in this country during the years of peace. What is particularly significant and remarkable in this spectacular artistic renaissance—for it is nothing less—is the difference between the new public and the pre-war public. The average age of the typical Queen's Hall or Wigmore Hall audience in former days would probably have been 40–50; to-day it is nearer 18–30—and I am assured, by those who are in a position to know, that this impression is borne out by actual statistics made by professional observers. It is precisely the younger generation that has become art- and music-conscious—and the majority of those who constitute this new audience are the very people of whom Mr. Orwell speaks —'the technicians and the highly paid skilled workers', etc. A short time ago I was fortunate in being able to be present at symphony concerts given by ENSA at Portsmouth and Southampton to war-workers and naval ratings. The choice of programme was uncompromisingly what it is customary to describe as 'highbrow', but the house was packed on both occasions, and the enthusiasm tremendous, beyond anything one could have expected in one's most optimistic dreams. Nothing like it would have been possible in pre-war days. It is not, I think, going too far to say that in such phenomena—for the particular experience cited is by no means an isolated or exceptional instance, but one which is reproduced daily throughout the country—we are entitled to perceive the beginnings of a veritable artistic revival in England. And, acutely disturbing though the conclusion may be in certain respects, one is reluctantly compelled to admit that it has to be attributed solely to the war. Without the war, indeed, it could never have come about. It is of the utmost importance that it should not be allowed to come to an end with the war, but that it should be maintained, fostered and further developed in the years of peace which lie ahead. Otherwise it will have been in vain.

The only disquieting feature in this re-birth of the spirit of music in this country—the greatest since the Elizabethan age—consists in the fact that it is largely confined to 'the classics'. In many ways this is a good thing, but the fact remains that if a genuine, healthy musical revival is to materialize, the creative artist must play his part no less than the public. It is not enough for the latter to become more sensitive and responsive; the former must be more forthcoming and accessible. The ever-widening schism between artist and public, the catastrophic 'splits' between the two interdependent limbs which has for so long been one of the leading characteristics of modern art, must be brought to an end, for it spells the death of art. The culminating point of this tendency is to be found in the *Finnegan's Wake* of James Joyce, which, apart

D

from a few isolated passages here and there, remains completely unintelligible to every one except the writer himself, who is now dead. In music we similarly find the *reductio ad absurdum* in the later work of Schönberg, which is similarly written for himself alone, apart from a steadily diminishing band of docile and credulous disciples.

In order to avoid misunderstanding on this point it will be as well to say here that we have no intention of suggesting that one kind of art is intrinsically better than another; that the form of art which appeals to millions is necessarily better than that which appeals to thousands, or that which appeals to thousands better than that which appeals to hundreds, and so on. A certain eminent music critic, Mr. Ernest Newman, once put forward the theory that no work of art which does not appeal to ' the plain man ' of its time is of any enduring value. We believe, on the contrary, that many admirable works of art appeal only to a few, and will continue to appeal only to a few, and are none the worse for that. There is no greater writer in the English language than Walter Savage Landor, but his audience is, always has been, and always will be, small. The heroes, the martyrs, and the saints of art, with their few devoted disciples, are as necessary and desirable as those with wider appeal and greater audiences. All we wish to suggest here is that what is necessary at this particular historical juncture is something different. The artist must for the time being, at least, descend from his god-like eminence in the clouds and take on mortality and walk among his fellow-men once more, even if it entails a certain loss of divinity. Contact must be re-established between the artist and the public, for we believe in the possibility of the redemption of man through art, and that life without art is not worth living.

In recent times the chief aim of the artist has been to achieve a recognizably individual utterance, to cultivate his personality. To-day, he should aim rather at cultivating his impersonality: those aspects of life and experience which he shares with others, rather than those which are his own unique possession, the things which unite rather than those which separate, the things which bind together—which is the original meaning of the word ' religion '.

It would even be a good thing if art were to become anonymous again, as it has been in other days. In the Middle Ages, for example, no one cared greatly to know who had painted the picture, written the music, designed the cathedral. The people, interested in art, were, rightly, not interested in the artist's personality. It was the work in itself, the *Ding an sich*, that mattered, and whether they liked it or not. Architecture in particular has always tended to be an anonymous art, and its decline coincides with the emergence of definite names and personalities. The names of very few of the architects of the great medieval churches are known, and no one pays much attention to them when they are.

' The custom of signing pictures originated with the growing importance of individuality in style. The primitives, whose art was communal, never signed their works. The twentieth century, on the other hand, has witnessed the apotheosis of the signature, when the picture may be little more than a scrawl around the magic name.' (*Sickert*, by Robert Emmons.)

In recent times the personality of the artist has become more important than his work. He is expected to do this or that, because he is he. Every artist, however great he may be, is bound to be adversely influenced by this shadow he drags about with him, cast by the sunshine of his fame and reputation. He is compelled to parade a consistent personality, and does not dare to be his spontaneous self lest it should seem to contradict his self of yesterday. Always to be expected to be oneself means that one has to be consistent, and no artist should ever be consistent.

Anonymity, on the other hand, gives freedom. The artist need fear no responsibility towards his *alter ego*, but can freely obey the impulse of the mood or the moment. He drops the mask, the *persona*,[1] and becomes his real spontaneous self. Anonymity, in fact, paradoxically enough, leads to an enlargement, an enhancement of individuality, whereas personality, in the ordinary accepted sense of the word, almost invariably tends to become a prison, a chain and fetters. Royalty, whenever it wishes to be free to do what it wants and to enjoy itself, travels *incognito*, so also should the royalty of the spirit.

[1] The Latin word *persona*, it is interesting and significant to note, means a player's mask.

Gabriele d'Annunzio, prince of lovers, used to say that his proudest conquest was that of a girl whom he picked up in the streets of Milan. When he mentioned his name, expecting her to be overcome, she had never heard of him. At first annoyed, he quickly realized that it was really a compliment; she had loved him for himself and not for his reputation of a famous man, like all his other conquests. Similarly, the proudest moment in an artist's life is, or should be, when someone says ' What a lovely picture ', or ' What a beautiful piece of music ', without looking for the signature on the picture or the name of the composer in the programme.

The fame which attaches to the personality rather than to the work of the artist is a false and meretricious thing, and many of those who achieve it spend most of their lives running away from it and seeking to escape it. Worst of all, he cannot live the life of a normal man, and without normal human contacts he cannot be an artist. The famous man who does not run away from it—Bernard Shaw is a good example—ceases to be either himself or an artist, and becomes merely a public bore, a pulpit orator. The artist should not be a public figure; it is not good for him, or for his art. He should live in the background, and seek to merge himself in the anonymous masses of his fellow men, or to live in solitude. Nothing more infallibly saps an artist's integrity than this kind of false fame which comes chiefly from newspaper publicity and social *réclame*. Few who experience it remain unscathed.

The plain truth of the matter is that the modern artist has got a bit above himself. He exalts himself at the expense of his art. He seems to think that he does it all himself, and that the world should be grateful to him and should bow down before him and worship him. Actually it is he who should be grateful for being allowed to become the humble and imperfect instrument of a divine purpose. It is no more he personally that performs the miracle of artistic creation than it is the village priest who causes transubstantiation in the ritual of the Mass. It is his function, not his person, which is worthy of reverence and admiration. Artists, like priests, considered simply as human beings, generally stand on a much lower level of decency than is to be found in any other walk of life. The company one meets in a four-ale bar in a public-house in Wapping is preferable any day to that which one encounters when a concourse of artists is gathered together. There is even much to be said for the view that artistic talent, or genius, is as much a disease of the human psyche as the pearl is of the oyster. The product is beyond price, but it would do many artists good if they could be induced to regard themselves as little better than diseased oysters.

Let us conclude these observations with a highly relevant quotation from an essay by Henry Miller entitled ' The Eye of Paris ', in the volume *Max and the White Phagocytes*:

> We have reached the point where we do not want to know any longer whose work it is, whose seal is affixed, whose stamp is upon it; what we want, and what at last we are about to get, are individual masterpieces which triumph in such a way as to completely subordinate the accidental artists who are responsible for them.

This, I firmly believe, will be the art of the future, of the immediate future—a form of art which will express and appeal to that which is fundamental and common to all, instead of, as in recent years, that which expresses a particular isolated personality and appeals only to a few. In a word, the artist must become again what he originally was, and what he was always intended to be: the servant of the public, and not its capricious and irresponsible master, and a person of low social status as in former times rather than the spoilt darling of the gossip column and the society salon of to-day. So little do we know of the private life and personality of the two greatest poets of all times, of the antique and modern worlds respectively, that modern criticism seeks to prove that neither of them existed, but that both are pure myths. No better example of the essential anonymity of the greatest art could be found than the life and work of Homer and Shakespeare. In music, Bach is a similar instance of impersonality.

It might perhaps be thought from what has been said above that Hindemith's *Gebrauchsmusik* was the ideal towards which composers should strive in the immediate future. Far from it. Whatever Hindemith's conceptions may be in theory, his practice is very different from what we have in mind. Hindemith writes music to order, ostensibly to satisfy a popular demand, but he does not satisfy it. There is no composer more disliked—rightly or wrongly—by

45

the ordinary concert goer, than Hindemith. What we want to see is precisely the opposite: the composer who writes what he wants to write and what will at the same time appeal to the ordinary concert-goer. By the 'ordinary concert-goer' we do not postulate an imaginary, disembodied ideal, but the audience which congregates at Promenade Concerts, or at Sadler's Wells in the days before the war. It is for such audiences and others like them, that we must primarily work in the years to come. In a word, the artist in the immediate future must come down to earth once more, as it were, and re-establish the vital contact with ordinary men and women which has been largely lost by his predecessors. The alternative is that of a few rare spirits functioning in a kind of vacuum, creating solely for themselves, or *ad majorem Dei gloriam*—a very fine ideal, one to be respected, admired, revered, but not what is imperatively demanded at the present moment.

What is it that this by no means ideal or abstract audience asks from music? First and foremost, as we have already said, enjoyment. As chief instrument of this enjoyment it demands melody; and by melody we do not mean merely fine melodic writing but what is vulgarly called tune. On the other hand it generally hates like poison recondite harmony without, however, being at all hidebound in this respect. Indeed, it is quite surprising what it can be induced to swallow by some composers, of whom Berg is a good example. But the reason for this is, that with all its surface obscurity of harmonic idiom, especially when studied on paper, with Berg the result in performance sounds very much like late Wagner, particularly certain pages in *Parsifal*. It is probably the chief flaw in Berg as an artist, in fact, that he so often seems to employ a new technique and vocabulary in order to achieve what can be achieved, and has already been achieved, by simpler and more orthodox means. The greatest art is rather that which seems to express something entirely new by means of a traditional technique; and this, I venture to suggest, is more likely to be the art of the immediate future than is that of Berg, or anything similar.

But Berg is an exception in his comparative popularity with the ordinary listener. Bartók, Schönberg, Webern, he cannot tolerate, nor probably will he ever be able to tolerate. He is, of course, wrong in this. As we have already said, we do not agree with Mr. Newman in regarding the plain man as the infallible arbiter in matters of art. There is much that is good and great that will probably always be above his head, and none the worse for that. But it is not what we want at the present time.

What has been said above is also applicable to rhythm. Writers on music talk very glibly and plausibly about ' the tyranny of the bar line ' and the monotony of the four-, eight- and sixteen-bar phrases of the classical masters, but the plain hard fact remains that at least nine-tenths of the greatest music, and ten-tenths of all that has achieved popularity, has been almost entirely built up in such symmetrical periods.

As necessary and fundamental conditions for the creation of a popular art, then, we postulate the restoration not merely of melody but even of tunefulness to a position of primary importance; the retrogression of harmonic experimentation into the background, and the predominance of comparatively simple and orthodox rhythmical structures. A certain strategical retreat, in fact, is indicated on the part of the composer, as compared with the art of the immediate past.

The essence of the matter is contained in a passage from the recently published *Letters to Dorothy Wellesley* by the late W. B. Yeats, the greatest poet of our time:

This difficult work which is being written everywhere has the substance of philosophy and is a delight to the poet with his professional pattern; but it is not your road or mine, and ours is the main road, the road of naturalness and swiftness, and we have thirty centuries on our side. We alone can think like a wise man, yet express ourselves like the common people. These new men are the goldsmiths working with a glass screwed into one eye, whereas we stride ahead of the crowd, its swordsmen, its jugglers, looking to right and left.

In these fine words a whole aesthetic is enshrined; the aesthetic of the art of the near future no less than that of the remote past. It is not, admittedly, the aesthetic of yesterday, but what is more dead than yesterday? It will be said, no doubt, that such a reversion to the ideals of the past amounts to an attempt to put the clock back, as the saying is, and that such an attempt is foredoomed to failure.

47

We shall only reply in the words of G. K. Chesterton who, when his opponent in an argument said ' You can't put the clock back ', replied, ' My dear Sir, you can. Watch me ', and going up to the mantelpiece he moved the hands of the clock back with his pudgy forefinger. And this is not merely being funny; it is profoundly true. Time is just what we choose to make it, a purely artificial concept. We put the clock forwards and backwards twice a year nowadays, as a matter of course: and it is equally easy in other spheres—easier in fact. People who say that one cannot put the clock back are merely obsessed with the outmoded, evolutionary conception of everything progressing in a straight line, inevitably, inexorably. Things never do, and history is full of instances in which the clock has been put back. And the best of all possible reasons for putting it back is when it has obviously been going too fast. There are also occasions when it is good to put it forward, when it has been going too slow, but just at the moment it must be put back.

In actual fact it might be truer to say that, owing to a defect in the mechanism, the hands of the clock have been travelling backwards instead of forwards for some time, and that the adjustment it is now proposed to make is, in reality, a setting of them in motion in the right direction once more. At the outset of this essay it was observed that after 1914–18 everything seemed to resume as if nothing particular had happened, and in a sense this is true enough; i.e. things started off again where they had left off, but they also started running backwards, and have continued to do so ever since. It is no mere coincidence that during the inter-war years all the catchwords and slogans of successive art movements centred in a ' back to ' something or other. They have all been retrogressive, not merely in intention, but in fact. Most of what has in recent years passed for being the last word in modernity and contemporaneity has been purely reactionary. We have experienced the odd sensation of travelling backwards in time, as if mounted on the Time Machine of H. G. Wells's imagining, through a landscape we have already seen. The roaring 20's are really surprisingly like the naughty 90's, when you look at them closely, and the most seemingly modern of all modern movements, the one left ultimately in possession of the field—surrealism—is quite demonstrably, and even avowedly, a reversion to the early romantic world of Horace Walpole, Maturin, and Monk Lewis in England; de Nerval, Petrus Borel (*le Lycanthrope*) and the young Théophile Gautier in France; of Hoffmann, Brentano and Chamisso in Germany; expressed in a style of painting which would have reflected great credit on the Royal Academy of a century ago.

It is as if, with 1914, culture and civilization and art had recoiled, like a wave from a breakwater. We have retrogressed about a century in the last twenty-five years. The dizzy rate of movement that we observe in the last quarter of a century has been uniformly backwards; and in reversing the hands of the clock from the direction in which they have been travelling, we are in reality setting them in forward motion once more.

To return: the audience which is to constitute the nucleus of the post-war audience for which we must primarily work, is that represented by these two institutions—the Promenade Concerts and Sadler's Wells—under normal peace-time conditions. It is a significant fact, incidentally, and no mere coincidence, that both of them have been gradually built up on that basis of *gusto*, or popular appreciation, which, earlier in this essay, we have seen to be the foundation of all sound and healthy aesthetic experience. Both began in the most humble and unpretentious way: the Promenade Concerts with programmes of operatic *potpourris* and sentimental ballads; the ' Old Vic ' with *Maritana*, *The Bohemian Girl*, and so forth. They would never have achieved what they have achieved without these humble origins. The growths of art, like those of nature, require manure in order to flourish. The loveliest lily is that which springs from the richest dung-heap.

The Promenade Concerts are essentially a national institution, like the National Gallery, performing the same function for music that the latter performs for the art of painting. It should equally be a permanent institution, functioning all the year round. This is not as impracticable as it might seem at first sight. If it is possible to fill a hall in August and September, when, in normal times, most people are away on holiday, it should be all the more possible to fill it at other times of the year. It would only be necessary to extend the season gradually, year by year, starting a little earlier and finishing a little later until the annual circle is completed. A decided and resolute step in this direction was taken in 1944 when the Promenade Concerts started operations in June, playing to as large houses as when they started a month or two later. The Albert Hall should become the permanent, perennial home of the Promenade Concerts. In the first place, it is the proper psychological locality for a national museum; and in the second place, it is unsuitable for any other concerts, and ideal for the rough and ready, unpolished, but adequate performances which are all that are conceivable under such conditions as those which necessarily prevail in such an institution as the Promenade Concerts, in view of the manifest impossibility of giving adequate rehearsals, from an epicurean point of view, to daily performances such as these.

For this reason, so far from agreeing with those who are wont to complain that too few contemporary novelties are performed in the programmes, I am rather of the opinion that there are too many, that there should not be any at all. Firstly, it is unfair to a new work and its composer to present it without a degree of rehearsal which is unobtainable under the conditions which prevail; and it is equally unfair to the audience. The Promenade Concerts, in fact, should constitute a permanent repository of classical masterpieces, like the National Gallery, and nothing else: with Sadler's Wells performing the same function with regard to the musico-dramatic side of the repertory. Modern novelties should be omitted, for they are not wanted. With all the admirable and desirable qualities of *gusto* and enthusiasm which characterize the audiences of these two institutions, it has to be admitted and accepted that their taste is in the main unadventurous and conservative. (The Sadler's Wells ballet audience is, of course, an entirely different one from the operatic, clamouring for novelties to the same degree as the latter fights shy of them.)

The fact remains that without new works, fresh blood, there can be no healthy musical life. We need, therefore, another institution, a musical equivalent to the Tate Gallery, which will concern itself exclusively with the presentation of new and contemporary work, on the lines of the Contemporary Music Concerts given by the B.B.C. in the years before the war. It cannot be too strongly emphasized that some such institution is an absolute necessity, for ultimately there is no hope for music in a community which enjoys no contemporary creative life of its own, but subsists entirely or overwhelmingly in the past, as in this country.

To this it will no doubt be objected that there is already a vast amount of vital creative activity in our midst, and that British composers to-day are at least equal, if not positively superior, to those of any other country at the present time. It would give us great pleasure to be able to subscribe to this opinion, but we regret to say that we cannot. The fact that English music is in a very much healthier condition to-day than it was half a century ago does not necessarily mean that we are now on top of the musical world, as so many people fondly imagine and loudly proclaim. Actually the number of composers here who can be considered up to European standards could be counted on the fingers of one hand.

It is necessary to say this quite frankly, because in this, as in so many other things, there is a danger in our national vice of complacency. We have praised and encouraged the native composer so much and for so long that he has began to lose his sense of proportion and to develop a swollen head. One observes precisely the same phenomenon in dealing with dwarfs, cripples and hunchbacks. Everyone is so kind and helpful, so tactful and sympathetic, that they almost invariably end up by becoming fantastically arrogant and conceited—and so it has been with the British composer. We have told him for so long that he is as good as anyone else, in order to encourage him, that he now honestly believes he is better than anyone else. The time has come for a slight corrective.

This is not to say that one is pessimistic or cynical as regards the future of music in this country. On the contrary, the prospects were never so bright. If it is true that, as already suggested earlier in these pages, too great material prosperity and affluence is the enemy, not the friend of art, both in the individual and in the community, both in creator and public—well, that is a state of affairs which is being rapidly remedied, it will surely be agreed. If the cult of the English Gentleman and the old-school-tie is the greatest enemy to artistic achievement in this country—well, that is going too, if, indeed, it has not already gone. If smug, complacent self-satisfaction and arrogance is the besetting sin of our island race, and the chief obstacle to its artistic development—well, it has had some nasty shocks lately, and it looks like getting some more in the near future.[1] In *Predicaments*, written some years before the war, I ventured to suggest that a military or naval defeat or two might administer a salutary jolt to the national soul. Well, we certainly have had them. There is even a distinct possibility that we shall have a dangerously enlarged soul by the time we are finished, even when we ultimately win the war.

It has been suggested above that the two most vital and deep-rooted institutions in pre-war English musical life are the Promenade Concerts and the Vic-Wells Opera, and it is to be hoped that they will continue to flourish in the post-war world. They represent the nucleus of our musical future, always provided, of course, that their functioning is confided to the right hands. But over all activities there looms the portentous, menacing, Brocken apparition of the British Broadcasting Corporation, on whose knees rests the major part of the present fortunes of music in this country—a proportion, moreover, which is more likely to increase than diminish in the immediate future. Any attempt to determine this future must therefore take into consideration the nature and extent of the activities of this vast and potent organization.

On the credit side let it be said straightway that the musical world owes a deep debt of gratitude to the B.B.C. for many things it has accomplished in the course of its existence. In the first place it has created what is undoubtedly the finest orchestra in the country, and, secondly, it has always gone out of its way to present works which otherwise, on account of their prohibitive demands, artistic and financial, would in all probability never have been heard—such works, for example, as the *Gurrelieder*, *Erwartung*, and the *Variations* of Schönberg, the *Doktor Faust* of Busoni, Berg's *Wozzeck* and *Violin Concerto*, Milhaud's *Christopher Columbus*, Honegger's *King David*, van Dieren's *Chinese Symphony*, Constant Lambert's *Summer's Last Will and Testament*, the *Te Deum*, *Requiem*, and *Symphonie Funèbre et Trionfale* of Berlioz—to men-

---

[1] This was written before the advent of the flying bomb.

tion only a few titles at random—all chosen and presented without prejudice for or against any school or tendency. It may be said, of course, that such activities are part of its duty, and that it can well afford them. That is perfectly true, in the same way that it is true that Sir Hugh Lane, Mr. Samuel Courtauld, M. Eumorfopoulos and other art-patrons could well afford to build up their magnificent collections of works of art. The fact remains that not all wealthy men show a similar taste, discernment and generosity, and no other official institution in this country has ever done so much for the cause of music as the B.B.C., in the face of the most violent hostility on the part of the overwhelming majority of its Philistine subscribers. All honour where honour is due.

Unfortunately there is a formidable debit side to the account. On all sides, in every section of the musical community, whether composers, critics, singers, players, or the general listening public, there is a steadily mounting *crescendo* of dissatisfaction and irritation directed against the B.B.C. What is perhaps even more significant and remarkable is the fact that these adverse sentiments are whole-heartedly shared and endorsed by all the best minds—and there are many of them—within the organization itself. In G. K. Chesterton's satirical fantasy *The Man who was Thursday*, it will be remembered, a detective succeeded by a subterfuge in being elected a member of the inner circle of an international anarchist society, only to discover gradually that all his colleagues and associates were also policemen in disguise; similarly the adverse critic of the B.B.C. who comes into personal contact with the executive of the organization finds, to his astonishment, that not only do they agree with his criticisms for the most part, but they even go further in their denunciations. If you want to hear a really searing and withering indictment of the B.B.C. you do not have to go beyond its own portals. And in the strictures which follow it should be clearly understood that they are not directed against any individuals, but the institution, the machine, of which these individuals are themselves, as often as not, the first and chief victims.

The machine—that is the operative word, which explains what is wrong with the organization. From top to bottom all engaged in it seem to be in the grip of an impersonal machine, of which

53

they are the constituent parts, the cogs and wheels, but over which they exercise no control; and the average mentality which the machine exhibits is lower than that of any of the individuals comprising it. The operative power and direction can never be confronted, fought and overcome, because it is not vested in any definite tangible individual or group of individuals. To try to track it down to its lair is as desperate and hopeless an undertaking as the ' Hunting of the Snark ', of Lewis Carroll.

The B.B.C. is a machine, a bureaucratic machine. In certain aspects of its multifarious activities it no doubt has to be—in its vast news-service, and so forth. But the application of bureaucratic methods and Whitehall mentality to art is the cause of all the trouble, so far as music is concerned; and here we come back to the very point from which this essay started—the fatal confusion between art and politics in the modern world. At the head of affairs of State we find everywhere disgruntled and unsuccessful artists; in control of artistic activities we find everywhere inefficient and incompetent civil servants. The only rational and, in the long run, efficient form of political government is democratic, yet everywhere we find dictators or would-be dictators—they are all the same in every country. The only efficient form of government in matters artistic is dictatorial, yet everywhere we find art under the control of committees and civil servants, and the B.B.C. is the most flagrant example of this deplorable tendency. All its musical activities, admirable as they are in many ways, are vitiated by this Whitehall mentality. The B.B.C. Charter, I understand, comes up for reconsideration in a short time. It is to be hoped that some steps can be taken to dissociate the necessarily bureaucratic control of certain of its activities from that which quite unnecessarily and perniciously operates in the field of art and what can broadly be defined as ' entertainment '—otherwise the outlook, so far as music is concerned, in the B.B.C. is a gloomy one. What the musical department of the B.B.C. needs, above all things, is a single, dominating, dictatorial personality who knows what he wants, what the public wants, or should be given (which is not necessarily the same thing), and who knows how to get it—a musician, in fact, who is given *carte blanche*, and not merely a civil servant ' yes-man '.

The B.B.C., moreover, being essentially, as at present constituted, a bureaucracy is, like all bureaucracies, inevitably a hot-bed and breeding-ground of all the freemasonries enumerated earlier in this essay. The number of log-rollers, wire-pullers, back-scratchers and backstair-climbers who have managed to infiltrate into the organization by means of one or other of the forms of influence already enumerated, is truly impressive in its proportions. And of all forms of freemasonry in a bureaucracy, more potent and subtle than that of the freemasons themselves, of the Scots, the Jews, the public school and university gentry, stronger even than that of the homosexuals, stronger even than a combination of them all, is the invincible freemasonry of mediocrity—the trade union of the 'leetle peeple' of whom Frederick Delius used to speak, in his inimitable accent. Indeed, even such a chimerical, though perfectly possible, figure as a Scottish Jew who has been to Eton and Oxford and has homosexual leanings—even with all these qualifications and recommendations, he will find it difficult to obtain a footing inside the B.B.C. if he has any talent. However much the 'leetle peeple' may hate each other individually—and their capacity for hatred is the only big thing about them—whatever may be their personal rivalries and vendettas—and they are on a scale and a degree of internecine intensity without parallel save in Italy at the time of the Borgias—they spontaneously forget their personal differences, close their ranks, present a united front, and fight as one man against the potential advent into their midst of a rival of talent. That there are, and have been, many intelligent and highly competent personalities on the staff has been admitted, but they are almost inevitably thwarted by the overwhelming, omnipresent, dead-weight of self-seeking mediocrity. Unless, or until, a complete change of policy is carried through, this state of affairs is bound to continue, and the enormous potentialities in the cause of music which lie in the hands of this vast organization are doomed to failure and frustration. At the present moment it must reluctantly be admitted that the dead-hand of civil service bureaucratic control and organized mediocrity tends to increase rather than to decrease, but we are not without hopes for the future.

The most encouraging and inspiring feature of recent war-time

55

musical activities has been the increasing tendency towards de-centralization. It is, indeed, remarkable to contrast the state of unhealthy stagnation which prevailed in the musical life of the provinces prior to the war, with the vigorous impulse which now animates it. Before, all vitality, such as it was, centred round London, as in a heart which was too weak to pump the life-giving blood into the extremities; the provinces were for the most part cold and apathetic, suffering from progressive anaemia. To-day they are pulsing with warmth and vitality. Indeed, the most encouraging feature of the present musical renascence in England is precisely the evident determination on the part of the great provincial centres such as Manchester, Birmingham, Liverpool, Newcastle, Glasgow and others too numerous to mention, to possess a musical life of their own instead of relying more or less exclusively on that emanating from the capital. There could be no fairer omen for the future. When every large city in the kingdom has its own regular orchestra, choir, and everything else that goes with them, then, indeed, England may become again what she was in Elizabethan days, the most musical of European nations.

This process of revitalization and decentralization necessarily involves certain sacrifices. The general level of performance of the local organization, technically considered, is bound to compare unfavourably in many respects with that of a ' star ' orchestra from London which wanders about the provinces, repeating the same programme of familiar classics wherever it goes—a degenerate sur-vival of the old pre-war cult of the visiting foreign orchestra under a famous conductor with his own personal reading of Beethoven's Fifth Symphony, and so forth. Such performances, no doubt, had a technical finish, brilliance and subtlety to which no provincial, or even national, organization could aspire, but such activities are ultimately sterile, a form of Byzantinism, spelling the death of creative musical art. The perfect performance of the familiar classic, attended by an audience chiefly composed of the aristocracy and the plutocracy, as at Salzburg and Glyndebourne—nothing could be more destructive of music as a living art, reminding one of the homage paid by the courtiers of Don Pedro of Portugal to the lovely embalmed corpse of Inez de Castro.

And here, once more, and for the last time, our argument links up with a subject introduced and developed earlier in these pages— the *leit-motif*, indeed, of the whole essay. The days of such *de luxe* performances, as of the *de luxe* products in the creative sphere, are at an end. They belong to a past order, and will not recur again in our time. The future order will, beyond doubt, be of a ruder, rougher, but more vital order: music as an art, not for a small, select, exclusive clique of snobbish dilettantes, with exquisite and refined palates, but for the more crude and coarse, if you will, but more healthy and robust appetites of the masses. Communism, in fact, whether we like it or not, whether it becomes a political world-reality or not, has come to stay, for some time at least, in the world of art, and we had best make up our minds to accept the inevitable. But whether we like it or not, one thing is certain and undeniable, namely, that to-day we are witnessing a re-birth on a vast scale of an interest in and an enthusiasm for music on the part of the masses without parallel in modern times, in this country at least, and that this spectacular re-birth is due simply and solely to the war, as already observed above. The philosophic implications of this un-questionable fact are too deep and fundamental to be resolved within the modest limits of this essay. It is enough to say, in the words of de Quincey, in his prose poem *Savannah-La-Mar*, ' Less than these fierce ploughshares would not have stirred the stubborn soil '.

1943

Johannes Brahms

IT MAY safely be said without fear of contradiction that in no art are criteria and standards of criticism so narrow and circumscribed, and at the same time so uncertain and confused in their application, as they are in music. This melancholy state of affairs can probably be ascribed in large part to the curious predilection which musicians have always exhibited at regularly recurring intervals of time for forming themselves into two hostile and irreconcilable camps, neither of which will admit the existence of any redeeming feature in the other, or of any defect in itself.

However pardonable and even inevitable such intolerance may be in a creative artist, whose attitude towards his art must naturally be determined to a great extent by the nature of his own particular talent and largely coloured by his personal sympathies and prejudices, it is an attitude which is neither justifiable nor forgivable on the part of the critic, who ought to be something more than a docile camp-follower in the train of one or other of the warring factions which periodically distract musical history. For it is not as if broadmindedness and universality of outlook lead in the practice of criticism, as they are apt to do in creation, to a somewhat colourless eclecticism and lack of conviction. Precisely the contrary, they are a source of strength, not of weakness ; and the unchallengeable superiority of literary criticism at the present time over that of all the other arts is primarily due to its breadth and catholicity, to its tacit recognition of the fact that it is possible for two artistic manifestations to be diametrically opposed to each other and mutually irreconcilable without the acceptance of the one necessarily implying the rejection of the other. We no longer consider that the highest tribute of admiration we can pay to the genius of Shakespeare is to abuse and ridicule Racine, or that a taste for Baudelaire and Verlaine automatically precludes us from appreciating the very different qualities of Milton and Wordsworth. But in music everything is still regarded from the standpoint of tendency ; if we admire Beethoven we must despise Rossini, and the ability to appreciate Bartók or Schönberg is considered wholly incompatible with a love for Bach and Mozart.

It is surely time that musical critics learnt a lesson from their literary colleagues and adopted the wholesome principle of religious toleration ; abandoning once and for all this Ormuzd and Ahriman conception of art, and recognizing the truth that tendencies are in themselves nothing, that only works are good or bad, and that there are more roads than one which lead to Parnassus.

No composer has ever suffered more from the characteristic one-sidedness and narrow-mindedness of musical criticism than the subject of the present essay, and no better example could be found of the errors and misconceptions to which they inevitably give rise. On the one hand, he has been raised to a position of equality with the greatest masters of all time, in stature comparable only to Bach and Beethoven (for by the formula of the three B's even Mozart is implicitly disqualified from competing with him) ; on the other hand, he has been made the object of a relentless and vindictive vendetta, first by the Wagnerians during his lifetime and by the representative of modern tendencies since his death, according to which he is regarded as a symbol of everything that is most detestable and contemptible in musical art. There is this, however, to be said in partial extenuation of the latter point of view, that it has been almost entirely the result of the wholly disproportionate claims which have been put forward on his behalf. When one finds a critic writing airily, *en passant*, that ' *all* the themes of Brahms have the *finest* melodic curves that were *ever* devised in music ' (italics are ours), it is impossible not to experience a momentary irritation. Like begets like, and an exclusive and esoteric cult such as that of the Brahmsians could hardly fail to provoke an equally violent reaction as a natural consequence. Nevertheless, a cult has more to fear from the excesses of its followers than from persecution, however violent, and the experience of those who come eventually to entertain a respect and admiration for Brahms resembles that of the Jew in the tale of Boccaccio, who, on paying a visit to Rome and seeing there the wickedness and corruption of the priests, was forced to the conclusion that the religion which could endure and flourish in spite of such things must indeed be divine. And the fact that neither the opposition of his adversaries nor the infinitely more dangerous excesses of his adherents—not even the terrible works which have been committed in his name and under his influence—have succeeded in depriving Brahms of his secure hold on the affections of the large majority of intelligent musicians, or prevented him from continually making fresh converts, is in itself sufficient proof of the inherent vitality of his art.

The fact remains that this perpetual alternation between two extremes has done Brahms an incalculable amount of harm by creating a false perspective, the effect of which has been to exaggerate his merits unduly from the one point of view and his faults from the other, and effectually to conceal his true nature from both alike. In all the mass of literature which has grown up around his work it is virtually impossible to find anything approaching an impartial and discriminating estimate of its significance. He has fossilized into a kind of historical concept, a highly conventionalized lay figure, bearing little or no relation to actuality—a fate which is all the more extraordinary because there is so little justification for it. Brahms is not by any means either the saint or sinner that he is commonly represented to be; neither is he as simple a problem as he appears. Before we can hope to see him as he really is it will first be necessary to rid ourselves of any preconceived notions and historical prejudices which we may entertain concerning him.

For example, he has been so constantly painted by his admirers as a kind of musical Parsifal heroically resisting the insidious blandishments of Wagner-Klingsor and the seductions of Kundry-Liszt and the houris of Weimar, and restoring to its pristine purity the Holy Grail of the true musical tradition which had been sullied through the equivocal conduct of Schumann-Amfortas, that it is a distinct surprise to find that his early works reveal a quite marked sympathy with the lamentable tendencies which he is supposed to have been combating. Not only do they show manifest traces of the influence of the new school with respect to form, exemplified in his occasional adoption of the device of thematic transformation, i.e. the employment of the same theme in slightly different guise as the subject of separate movements in a work (see, for instance, the First Sonata for piano, in which the theme of the *finale* is derived from that of the first *allegro*, and the second, where the same subject is employed in both *scherzo* and *andante*), but also definite indications of a leaning towards that most pernicious of all heresies in the eyes of the orthodox—namely, programmatic or poetic tendencies. The andante of the third piano sonata is prefixed by a quotation from a poem of Sternau, the fourth movement, entitled *Rückblick*, is similarly based upon another poem of the same writer, ' O wusstest du, wie bald, wie bald ', etc., and the first of the Ballads, Op. 10, is also headed by a quotation from Herder's translation of the old ballad ' Edward, Edward '. The last two examples are not merely programme music in the ordinary sense of the word, in which the general mood and asmosphere of the music is suggested by the poem, but the very rhythms are dictated by the rhythm of the verse. They are, in fact, quite literally *Lieder ohne Worte*, songs without words, instrumental transcriptions of poems.

In fact, the general impression induced by a study of these works is one of a composer who, so far from being in any way hostile to the new ideas which were then being disseminated, was rather in sympathy with them, even to the extent of seeming to be a promising recruit to the ranks of the revolutionaries. That he was so regarded by the leaders of the movement is certain. Liszt invited him to Weimar with open arms, and Berlioz, writing to Joachim from Leipzig, says: ' Brahms a eu beaucoup de succès ici. Il m'a vivement impressionné l'autre jour avec son *scherzo* et son *adagio*. Je vous remercie de m'avoir fait connaître ce jeune audacieux si timide qui s'avise de faire de la musique nouvelle. Il souffrira beaucoup.'[1]

On the occasion of the first performance of the First Piano Concerto in D minor (written about the same time as the works mentioned, although not published until some time later) no one had a good word to say for Brahms except the Weimar school, and it was the conservative section of musical opinion which was most

[1] It is interesting to note that the only member of the Liszt party who regarded Brahms with suspicion and dislike was von Bülow, of all people. In a letter to Liszt he unburdened himself as follows: ' Pour moi ce n'est pas de la musique—que m'importent les Br's; Brahms, Brahmüller, Brambach, Bruch, Bragiel, Breinecke, Brietz ' ! Strange words, surely, from the future promulgator of the famous formula ' I believe in Bach, Beethoven and Brahms '. It is evident that whatever changes took place in von Bülow's opinions, he was at least constant in his echolalian obsessions.

uncompromisingly hostile, one representative organ going so far as to denounce it as a ' Dessert von schreienden Dissonanzen und mislautenden Klangen '.

Particular stress is here laid upon the romantic character of these early works, not merely because there has always been a tendency on the part of orthodox Brahmsians to ignore it as representing an aspect of their hero which it is difficult to reconcile with the particular conception of him which they wish to see established and accepted, but because it is a factor of the utmost importance in helping us to understand the true nature of his talent. Though these works may not be aesthetically as significant as many later ones, they are not by any means derivative as are the early efforts of most artists, or due to any extraneous influence. On the contrary, they are the expression of a very much more definite personality than many of the later works. Compare, for example, the bold and ardent Scherzo in E flat minor, in which Berlioz had found a spirit congenial to his own, with the flaccid and nerveless Serenade in D major for orchestra, Op. 11, which, as even an enthusiastic Brahmsian like Mr. Colles is compelled to admit, ' bows in turn to each classical predecessor, Haydn, Schubert, and the early Beethoven, and accepts unhesitatingly each convention of orchestration that they used '. There is no question as to which is the more individual work of the two. Indeed, it is difficult to realize that they were both written by the same man. They seem to have nothing in common, and to belong to entirely different worlds. It is a difference which cannot be explained by the mere interval of time which elapsed between them, for it is not a logical development, but a sudden *volte face*. Moreover, the change is not only sudden, unexpected, inexplicable; it is also curiously incomplete and not by any means permanent. It is like the intrusion of a new personality, without the departure of the old, which remains only momentarily in abeyance; a case of artistic possession in which two personalities strive for mastery without either ever completely gaining the upper hand. Brahms reminds one of the amusing satire of Mr. Aldous Huxley, in which the hero, normally a rather fastidious and intellectual young man, is at times possessed by the personality of a popular lady novelist. Similarly with Brahms, one is confronted alternately by the romantic composer of the songs and piano pieces, and the stern, uncompromising classicist of the first and fourth symphonies. He is a dual personality; with Faust he might say, 'Zwei Seelen wohnen, ach! in meiner Brust'. This is the explanation of the extraordinarily adverse and conflicting impressions which his works arouse in different people. By some he is reproached for his austerity and intellectualism; others find him too emotional and sentimental. He is alternately accused of a complete indifference to sensuous beauty and blamed for his luscious and cloying over-ripeness of sound. All these points of view are justified; they are all true of different works—sometimes of the same work.

This curious duality is highly characteristic of the German race, particularly at the time in which Brahms lived. What ostensible connexion is there between the Germany of, let us say, 1820, with its Brüderschaft clubs wherein young students, dressed in short black jackets and Byronic shirts and wearing top boots and long, flowing hair, holding a dagger in one hand and a quart tankard of beer in the other, drank to the radiant goddess of liberty, and the Germany of 1870, as exemplified in the arrogant militarist Prussian, with his pink, shaven head, high stiff collar, and aggressive bearing, who has become so painfully familiar to us of recent years? What is there in common between the Germany of Tieck, Hoffmann, and Novalis, and that of Bismarck and von Moltke; between the Rhineland with its ruined castles and vineyards and Loreley legends, and the monotonous, dreary plains of the Mark of Brandenburg? Nothing, seemingly—except, perhaps, the beer, the undying symbol of the Teutonic spirit. Germany is the Jekyll and Hyde among the nations, and every German is to some extent a microcosm, repro-ducing in himself the duality characteristic of his race. The reason why it is more noticeable in Brahms than in any other composer—except, perhaps, Richard Strauss—lies in the fact that he is probably the most completely and exclusively Teutonic artist who has ever lived. Many much greater poets and musicians may have come out of Germany, but for the very reason that they are greater they are not so representative. Goethe and Beethoven transcend all national limitations; Brahms, on the other hand, is the embodiment of the Teutonic spirit. Besides, it must be remembered that Brahms's life

63

was spent at the very time of the change from the old Germany to the new. The turning-point or climacteric of the race came with the failure of the revolutionary movement of 1848; from that time onward the old Germany was dead to all appearances, although the old romantic spirit still continued to subsist beneath the surface.

It is interesting to observe that this psychological duality has its exact counterpart in the physical development of Brahms. One might well be pardoned for imagining that the drawing of him at the age of twenty which figures in most of his biographies was purely imaginary, or at least highly idealized, if its characteristic traits were not so fully confirmed and substantiated by the descriptions of those who were intimate with him at the time. In the words of a young lady of his acquaintance, he was ' shy and retiring, modest and timid, of delicate appearance, with blue eyes and fair hair, and a voice like a girl, still unbroken, and a face like a child which a young girl could kiss without blushing (!) '—how are we to reconcile this romantic youth, the exact description of a hero out of Jean Paul or Novalis, with the later Brahms of coarse and rough appearance, the *senex promissa barba* of our Latin grammars, with his harsh voice and rude behaviour, who was in the habit of eating a whole tin of sardines with his fingers and pouring the oil down his throat? Fortunately, the change was not so complete and irrevocable in the spiritual as in the physical man, neither were its manifestations quite so disagreeable. Nevertheless, the parallel is a very striking one; for while, as we have already said, the music of Brahms in both its aspects typifies the German spirit, so in his physical personality in both phases he is the living embodiment of the racial type.[1]

Once this symbolical relation between Brahms and the national temperament has been grasped we are in possession of the key to the proper understanding of his art. It explains both its virtues and its defects. For while the German mind is essentially lyrical, contemplative, and philosophic, and fundamentally opposed to the heroic, the epic, and the monumental, it is at the same time adapt-

---

[1] His biographer Max Kalbeck tells us that he was regarded by ethnologists as a perfect example of the Teutonic type and that he even figured as such in a technical work on the subject.

ab'e and receptive to a quite remarkable degree, and capable of performing feats which are wholly foreign to its innermost nature; and the obsession of the modern German spirit by the ideal of the gigantic and the colossal—perhaps the most remarkable phenomenon in modern history—has its counterpart in the arts. One sees the beginning of it in the music of Brahms as clearly as one sees the end of it in the music of Strauss and Mahler.

And so we find throughout almost all the work of Brahms the sharp antithesis between his essentially gentle and quiescent temperament with its predominant mood of retrospective and wistful melancholy, and the perpetual striving after the ideal of a grandiose, neo-classic art which constantly impelled him to desert the smaller lyrical forms in which he was an accomplished master, in favour of the larger orchestral forms to which his talents were not so much unequal as fundamentally unsuited. For in the first place the symphony, or at least its initial movement, is essentially a dramatic form. Both in its derivation from the old dance forms and in its consummation in Mozart and certain works of Beethoven, its characteristic feature is the contrast and opposition of two dominant themes; the first strong and masculine, the second gentle and feminine—the Yin and Yang of Chinese cosmology, the generative principles of the universe. The whole development of the work is the outcome of the interaction of these two strongly contrasted principles; between them they beget the whole course of the movement. The development section is, so to speak, the child of the union of two musical sexes.

Now, Brahms could never write a great first movement in the classical style, along the lines of the conventional two-theme structure, because he was unable to invent strong and vital first subjects; in their place are generally found thinly disguised variants of second subjects. They are either arid and sterile as in the First Symphony, intermediary and hermaphroditic as in the Third, or frankly feminine as in the Second; and their relations with the second themes are consequently unproductive.

An explanation of this inability to conceive a strong first subject is to be found in a remark which he once made to his friend Dietrich, that whenever he wished to compose he thought of some folk-song,

65

and then a melody presented itself. Hence the lyrical, *volkstümlich* character of all his finest subjects; hence their lack of differentiation and variety. They all seem to conform to a folk-song archetype, and Brahms nearly always fails when he attempts the dramatic, classical, two-theme form because the folk-song type of melody is fundamentally unsuitable as its material basis. This is pretty generally recognized to-day. On the other hand, it is equally unsuited to the romantic symphonic poem form, which is based upon the formal principle of a single subject from which the whole organism evolves, as in the fugue and in many of the works of Beethoven's last period. The typical Brahmsian melody is as little susceptible of spontaneous generation as of dual reproduction.

Consequently, one finds that the form of Brahms's most successful first movements, such as those of the Violin Concerto, Violin Sonatas in A and G, and the Second Symphony, is neither that which we are accustomed to call classic nor romantic, neither symphonic nor fugal, based neither upon the principle of unity nor on that of duality, but of multiplicity; in these works the form ceases to be dramatic and epic, without becoming a monologue or a soliloquy. For example, in the first movement of the Violin Concerto one could count some twenty or more thematic fragments of a very similar character; they do not engender the course of the movement with each other, but are rather separate aspects of some archetypal melody; free variations or improvisations on a theme withheld; successions of lyrical episodes, like a sonnet sequence or a poem written in stanzas. Each part is a separate organic whole, but they are all so dexterously and cunningly welded together that it sometimes seems as if they did actually evolve from each other. Nevertheless, if one takes the trouble to examine such cases closely, one will generally find that some little figure or other has been surreptitiously smuggled into an episode out of that which is to succeed it, and artfully concealed until the moment for its appearance. In more homely terms, the rabbit is in the hat all the time. Not that it is necessarily any the worse for that; my intention is only to show that Brahms is, formally speaking, neither the classic master nor the *manqué* romantic of the Liszt school that he is alternately represented to be. He is at his best when he is neither one nor the other, but simply himself. He occupies a position apart from both schools, and it is only an historical accident that is responsible for the false conception of him which prevails to-day. In 1853, the year in which Robert Schumann's article appeared in the *Neue Zeitschrift für Musik*, proclaiming the advent of a new master in the person of Brahms, then a young man of only twenty years of age, musicians were still accustomed to the idea of a kind of apostolic succession of great masters, stretching back in a long and unbroken line into the dim and distant past, whose authority, handed down from one to the other as from father to son, no one could venture to dispute or disobey without incurring the suspicion of heresy and the penalty of excommunication. But with the death of Beethoven the direct line appeared for the time being at least to have come to an abrupt conclusion, and the behaviour of the musical world was as pathetic and ridiculous as that of a faithful dog who has lost his master and is trying to find him again in a crowd of strangers. The most unlikely people were rapturously greeted by the poor animal—composers as far apart as Mendelssohn and Meyerbeer were hailed on their appearance as the long-lost heir to the classic tradition.

It all seems very absurd to us to-day. Actually, of course, no great master ever has a successor, but only imitators, for the very simple and obvious reason that his work is, humanly speaking, perfect, and consequently not susceptible of further development. The great master is an end in himself, a completion and a triumphant consummation; only artists of the second rank, who suggest more possibilities than they are capable of realizing and exhausting, ever have successors. Neither Bach nor Palestrina has any at all; the real successor of Mozart is not Beethoven but Spohr, that of Wagner is not Strauss but Goldmark or Bungert. And Brahms has everything to gain and nothing to lose by the abandonment of the claims which have been put forward on his behalf to be regarded as the heir to the classic succession, for it only serves to concentrate attention on that aspect of his work which is least characteristic of him, in which he is at his worst, and causes his real gifts to pass unrecognized or insufficiently appreciated.

Unfortunately, there is little doubt that the Schumann article and the subsequent von Bülow formula of the three B's exercised a disastrous influence on Brahms himself and gave him a quite wrong idea of the real nature of his own talents, of the direction in which his real strength lay. He was perpetually trying to live up to a false ideal. He is like a man grappling with a task beyond his powers. It is this more than anything else which is responsible for the curious impression which so many of his less successful works arouse in the listener—an impression quite different from that produced by any other music, and one which it is very difficult to express in words. The First Symphony, for example, and particularly the introduction to the first movement, with its atmosphere of gloomy apprehension and its sombre and restless straining after something just out of reach, recalls the sensations which we experience in that familiar type of dream in which we are continually trying to run away from something, but in spite of our desperate efforts only get slower and slower until in the end we are crawling on our knees. Brahms certainly felt that he was a classicist, but at the same time was under no illusions as to the degree of success which had attended his efforts. Speaking to a friend named Koessler shortly before his death, he said: ' I know very well what place I shall eventually take in musical history; the same place as that which Cherubini occupies—that is my fate, my destiny.' But however true this may be of the one aspect of his work, he certainly does himself less than justice on another side, the side represented by the piano works and the songs.

Actually it would be difficult to think of any composer whose mentality was less akin to the classic spirit. He had an entirely false idea of what it was, and how it was to be attained. Classic art is not austere; its spirit is pre-eminently sensual and full of joy in the physical aspect of things. Mozart, perhaps the only real classicist in all music, is the very reverse of ascetic. No composer is so pre-occupied with sheer physical loveliness of sound for its own sake. But it is so in all great classical art. Many so-called admirers of the ' Greek spirit ' would be horrified if they could see the Parthenon as it really was, with its brightly painted statues, and its colossal chrys-elephantine figures, or were to find themselves on the Athenian Hampstead Heath during a Dionysian orgy. Yet one is perpetually hearing of the truly ' classical austerity ' and ' disdain of mere sensuous beauty ' in the symphonic music of Brahms. These qualities are certainly there, but they are the reverse of classical. As well call a desert anchorite an admirer of the Greek spirit as call the Brahms of the Fourth Symphony a classicist. Indeed, in his more austere and uncompromising mood Brahms reminds one strongly of Paphnuce, the monk in M. Anatole France's master-piece, *Thaïs*, who imagined that when he was heroically struggling with the temptations of the flesh he was struggling with the devil, whereas it was really God who had sent them in the hope of bringing him to a more reasonable frame of mind and a more natural mode of life. On the contrary, it was the devil who induced him to perform what he thought were pious acts, such as sitting on the top of a high pillar for many days and nights. And the spirit of sensuous beauty which Brahms was continually striving to overcome in himself, so far from being the devil, was the true classical spirit.

Fortunately for himself and us, his lapses from grace and right-eousness were frequent and often prolonged. As a rule it will be found that his severe mood, like that of Flaubert, another Saint Anthony, is succeeded by a reaction in the opposite direction; a spell of hair-shirts and matutinal scourgings is followed by a spell of self-indulgence. And so we find the period which culminated in the rigours and asperities of the First Symphony succeeded by a long interlude in which were produced the Violin Concerto, the second Piano Concerto, the Sonata for Violin and Piano in G, and the Second Symphony, all of which are among the most popular and accessible of his larger works. Similarly, the grim and arid Fourth Symphony, at which even many of the faithful draw the line, was followed by the splendid Quintet for Strings in G, the lovely clarinet Quintet, and the last piano works. So, in miniature, the same tendency can be observed throughout his development; after the stern F minor Quintet for strings and piano come the bright and vigorous, almost un-Brahmsian Paganini Variations; the for-bidding E minor 'Cello Sonata is succeeded by the Waltzes and the Horn Trio; and the Liebeslieder follow closely on the heels of the Requiem, and certainly, in this case at least, love proves stronger than death.

69

The Requiem has always been considered one of the landmarks in the music of Brahms, a view to which I have never been able to subscribe. Despite all its undoubted earnestness and sincerity, it fails to convince. The true religious spirit which redeems the frequent theatricality of the sacred works of Verdi and Liszt is lacking in it; it lacks faith, without which the eternal verities of life and death are apt to become tiresome platitudes. It does not need Herr Kalbeck to tell us that neither when Brahms wrote the Requiem nor even later in life did he believe in the immortality of the soul; one can see it clearly enough in every bar of the music. Piety without faith, reverence without belief, are not enough in a work of this kind. It is instructive to compare it with the Requiem of Delius; in the one the assertion of pious thoughts leaves one cold and unmoved; in the other the denial of the existence of a future life seems to receive a contradiction in the consoling and tender strains of the music. One might say of the Requiem, and, indeed, of many other works of Brahms, what Saint John the Divine said of the church of Ephesus: ' I know thy works and thy labour, and thy patience, and how thou canst not bear them which are evil. Nevertheless I have somewhat against thee, because thou hast left thy first love. Remember therefore from whence thou art fallen, and repent, and do the first works.' And in his last years Brahms did so. *On revient toujours à son premier amour*—how very true it is, in art as in life! How often one finds an artist returning in his last works to the spirit of his early ones! Berlioz returns in Les Troyens to his first love, Gluck; the last picture Gauguin painted in Tahiti was a Breton landscape, recalling his earliest works; and so Brahms in the end, particularly in the groups of piano pieces, Op. 116 to 119, seems to recapture something of the youthful romantic mood, with an added mellowness and serenity. In the collection of Volkslieder which he made in the last years of his life the last number is a vocal arrangement of the melody in the andante of his first sonata, his Op. 1, and possibly the first piece of music he ever wrote; in his own words, ' The last of the Volkslieder and the same in my Op. 1 constitute the snake with its tail in its mouth, signifying symbolically that the story is finished '—and symbolical it certainly is that both his first and his last utterance should emphasize so strikingly the most characteristic feature of all his best work, namely, its lyrical, singing quality, its ultimate derivation from song. For it is as a song-writer that he is perhaps greatest. It is true that he may not attain quite to the heights which Schubert does in a small handful of unexcelled masterpieces, but with this one glorious exception it is difficult to see whom one could place above him. Schumann, for example, although he undoubtedly wrote many fine songs, was, on the whole, of too introspective a turn of mind to be able to enter completely into the poet's conception. Too often the poem is for him merely the starting point of a series of purely personal meditations. Like the crystal or coloured disc which the clairvoyant or mystic employs in order to hypnotize himself, the poem is not an end in itself, but only the means to an excursion into the nebulous and misty depths of his inner consciousness.

Hugo Wolf represents precisely the opposite tendency. He possesses all the qualities which Schumann lacks. In the words of one of his most distinguished and consistent admirers, namely, Mr. Ernest Newman, ' He allowed the poet to prescribe for him the whole colour and shape of a song, down even to the smallest detail. . . . He set his face sternly against the suspicion of mere music-making. . . . Wolf may not have had the exquisite disinterested loveliness of Schubert, or the same vision of the light that never was on sea or land, but he indubitably had a deeper comprehension of men and the world, a greater breadth of sympathy, a keener probe of psychology, and a more consummate flexibility of style.'

This puts the case both for and, unconsciously, against Hugo Wolf as well as it can be done. These are the reasons which induce Mr. Newman to put him ' at the head of the song-writers of the world '—above even Schubert; they are the reasons which lead others, including myself, to relegate him with all due respect to a place in the second rank. Psychological probe, the understanding of the ways of this wicked world, and so forth, may be very estimable possessions, but they are not qualities which will enable a composer to become a good or even a tolerable song-writer, any more than they can make a good portrait painter. It is only too palpably true that the Hon. John Collier has admirably realized the type of the strong, silent man, and the type of the tender, clinging woman who have between them made the British Empire the peculiar thing that it is; it is true that Mr. Sargent in the Wertheimer series has admirably depicted the types who are making it what it will probably be in a few years' time, and building Jerusalem in England's green and pleasant land; but these worthy achievements do not, in my humble opinion, make either of them a great painter. It is the ability to handle a brush, not psychological insight, that makes Sargent, if not an artist of the front rank, at least one worthy of our attention; it is Collier's inability to do so, not by any means his sentimentality—no one could be more sentimental than Raphael —that makes him unworthy of our attention.

Ultimately, a poem is a pretext for music in the same way that, as far as the purposes of art are concerned, a model is a pretext for a painting, and no amount of psychological or even physiological penetration can make up for bad painting or inferior music. And our complaint against Wolf is, that with all his veracity and ability to enter into the spirit of a poem, he seldom succeeds in giving us just that one thing which we ask from a song, namely, good music —or, if Mr. Newman prefers it, ' mere music-making '.

The great song-writers understood this perfectly well; for them ' the music's the thing '. A song of Brahms is not, as a rule, as a song of Wolf so often is, a mere turgid flow of notes without any intrinsic value apart from the poem, but a delicately organized and articulated structure with a logic of its own. As long as he has succeeded in preserving the correct accentuation and declamation, Wolf is generally satisfied; his songs are often common-place and deficient in musical interest and undistinguished in style and workmanship. Brahms, on the other hand, was never content until he had created a vocal line of intrinsic melodic beauty and an accompaniment as full of musical subtlety as he could make it.

Admittedly, the music must have some relation to the poem, as the portrait must to the model. A great portrait painter does not merely express his own feelings, any more than he confines himself to the accurate reproduction of his sitter's features. The picture is a kind of collaboration. Here and there a characteristic trait is slightly exaggerated, there another is omitted or left unemphasized, in order that the conception of the whole can be realized. So in the music of the great song-writers one may occasionally find a faulty accentuation; words may sometimes be repeated for some purely musical purpose whereby the poetic sense may perhaps suffer slightly, but these are only details which are sacrificed in order to contribute to the greater beauty of the whole. Wolf is almost always too preoccupied with the features in detail to see the face as a whole; he often seems to work from line to line, from word to word, and fails to achieve formal unity and coherence. Certainly there are limits to the liberties which one is permitted to take with a poem, a point at which the logical conclusion would be to make the work a purely instrumental piece, and it is precisely Schumann's inability to get outside himself, and his tendency to turn a song into a piano piece with vocal accompaniment that excludes him from the very first rank of song-writers. He lacks objectivity of outlook, and resembles the portrait painter who is only successful with certain types with which he is in personal sympathy.

But to object, as many people do to-day, to a misplaced accent or faulty declamation as being a ' violation of the poem ', or a symptom of ' insensitiveness to poetic beauty ' is no whit less non-sensical than to complain that a painter who gives a lady a slightly longer nose in his picture than she actually possesses is guilty of a crime against humanity or thereby stands condemned as being insensitive to female beauty. On the contrary, it is rather the photographic artist and the musician ' who allows the poet to pre-scribe for him the whole shape and colour of a song ' that give proof of their lack of appreciation of poetic and human beauty, by their naive assumption that they can supply to the original some quality that it lacks. A good poem is a complete work of art, from which nothing can be taken and to which nothing can be added; it is simply a piece of gratuitous impertinence for a musician to imagine that he is capable of improving it. Respect for a poem would be more truly shown by abstaining from setting it to music at all, than by using it as a prescription for a musical work ' down to the smallest details '—a procedure that may be all very well in a dispensing chemist, but has little to do with either music or poetry. A song is as much a musical form as an opera; it is not a poem set to music

F

any more than an opera is a drama set to music. A good poem, like a good play, can only be spoilt by the addition of music; it cannot be improved upon. Song and opera are as different from poetry and drama as chalk is different from cheese; the best poems for music, like the best *libretti*, are those which afford the musician the fullest scope and the least hindrance to his purely musical purposes. To commend Wolf for only setting the best poems to music is like praising a composer who would only make operas out of the best plays. So far from being a sign of good taste, this merely shows that he had no understanding of the true nature of the art of song-writing, and if we place Brahms far above Wolf and Schumann it is largely on account of his thorough understanding of the form with which he is dealing, and because of his remarkably sure instinct in choosing the right poems.

It is not merely by virtue of a small handful of choice favourites that Brahms takes his high position among song-writers, but by the extraordinarily large mass of fine numbers—in actual amount possibly less than in the case of Schubert, but in an infinitely higher proportion to his output. It is perfectly true that other composers besides the latter may have equalled and even excelled him on occasions; a small handful of songs by Moussorgsky, Borodin, Debussy, possibly even one or two of Strauss, may be as good or even better than anything Brahms ever did, though this is very doubtful. One can at least concede that they possess a quality of imagination and sensitiveness to which Brahms cannot lay claim. But what is certain is this: that if a musical Palgrave were to set about making a Golden Treasury of songs, excluding, of course, operatic arias and vocal works of large dimensions, he would prob-ably find that he would have to include a greater number of examples by Brahms than by any other composer with the exception of Schubert; in precisely the same way, in fact, that the actual Palgrave gave a larger proportion of space to Wordsworth than to any other poet of his time. That is not to say that Brahms is necessarily greater, or even anything like as great as many of his contemporaries, any more than it means that Wordsworth was greater than Keats or Shelley, but simply that in such a test one is judging him on his own ground ,where he is at his best and greatest, instead of on the wider ground of the large orchestral forms, where he is at a disadvantage in competing with such giants as Berlioz, Liszt, and Wagner.

There is no doubt that there are many striking analogies between Brahms and Wordsworth. After a youth of ardent romantic enthusiasm they both cooled down very suddenly into a premature middle age, and in the bitter reproaches levelled at the former by the younger generation of musicians during his lifetime one finds an echo of the disillusionment of Wordsworth's former admirers on account of what seemed to them his apostasy. In the words of Browning,

> He alone breaks from the van and the freemen,
> He alone sinks to the rear and the slaves.

Again, both were made the object of an exaggerated worship and adulation, and both have paid dearly for it, by provoking the ridicule and obloquy of their antagonists. Both wrote a vast amount of second-rate and uninspired work, particularly in the larger forms. Their reputations will ultimately rest on their work in smaller fields—Wordsworth's on the *Lyrical Ballads* rather than on the *Prelude* or the *Excursion*, that of Brahms on his songs and piano pieces rather than on his symphonies or his *Requiem*. They are both lyrical, contemplative, and philosophic in temperament, and fail when they attempt the epic, the dramatic, or the passionate. They are alike incapable of the *allegro con brio* or the *prestissimo*; they lack *tempo*. Brahms is representative of everything that is most German, Wordsworth of everything that is most typically English. But there was in the latter a certain calm, mild grandeur, and ruggedness, as if something of his beloved lakes and mountains had entered into him. On the contrary, there is a distinct stuffiness and lack of fresh air in a great deal of Brahms's music. He preferred Vienna and the Prater to walking on the mountain-tops, and Baden-Baden, where, as Kalbeck says, 'Die Natur stand wie ein wohlgeordneter Tisch für ihn gedeckt '—with its civilized forests ' Wo kein erstickendes Unterholz, kein abgefallenes durres Laub, geduldet wurde ', to the wilder grandeur of the Black Forest.

It is, of course, largely on account of his nationality and because he so completely typifies the German spirit that there is a wide-spread tendency at the present day to depreciate Brahms unduly; but it also happens that there is also a purely artistic reaction against everything that he stands for. Our Zeitgeist is different, that is all; and there is no reason to suppose that it will be permanent. But although we of to-day admittedly do not find in his music the expression of our innermost thoughts and aspirations, that is no reason why we should refuse to tolerate and even sympathize with different ideals and different qualities of mind. Criticism, after all, and appreciation for that matter, ought to be something more than a mere chasing of our own tails or a self-satisfied contemplation of our own features in a mirror, and those who take the trouble to look for them will find in Brahms many qualities without which music would be very much the poorer, and many works which are destined to endure long after the music of most of our contemporaries has lost the transitory interest it has for us at the present day.

1923

Franz Liszt

THE PRESTIGE of a universally accepted dogma is often so great that it is exceedingly difficult, even for the most alert and discriminating critic, to throw off its hypnotic influence and arrive at an independent point of view. It is, indeed, somewhat depressing, though none the less highly salutary, to consider what a large proportion of one's habitual standards of judgement consists merely of prejudices and preconceived notions, so hallowed by tradition and sanctified by incessant repetition as to have attained to the status and dignity of incontrovertible truths. In many cases we maintain and give utterance to them unthinkingly, merely because it has never even occurred to us to question them.

Suppose, for example, that one were to ask any average intelligent music-lover for his opinion concerning the music of Palestrina. One can be perfectly certain that he would straightway begin to discourse eloquently and reverently upon its wonderful simplicity and perfection of style, its depth of devotional sentiment, and so forth; but if one were then to ask him what works of Palestrina he knew or had even only casually heard, it is exceedingly improbable, to say the least, that he would be able to mention the name of any one, except perhaps that of the *Missa Papae Marcelli*, and still more improbable that he would even recognize this if he were to hear it, or that he would be able to distinguish it from the work of any of Palestrina's innumerable predecessors, contemporaries, or successors who wrote *a cappella* Church music. Even the few critics and scholars—and how few they are!—who are sufficiently acquainted with his music to be entitled to an opinion concerning it are inevitably influenced to an incalculable extent in their judgement by the formidable prestige conferred upon it by centuries of unremitting and enthusiastic praise.

A similar example of precisely the opposite order is afforded by the music of Liszt, the mere mention of whose name is enough to evoke in response a string of epithets such as fustian, tinsel, pinchbeck, rhodomontade, tawdry, shoddy, garish, bedizened, and so on; but you will generally find that those people who are most lavish in their employment of this vocabulary know just as little of Liszt's music as the conventional admirers of Palestrina do of his. Even those who do know his work sufficiently well to be in a position to judge it for themselves almost invariably approach it with an adverse prejudice against it which is none the less, perhaps all the more, strong because it is to a great extent quite unconscious, the outcome of several decades of steady vituperation of Liszt on the part of musicians of every conceivable creed and tendency. The inevitable result is that they find in it precisely what they expect to find, what they have been taught to find, what they subconsciously wish to find.

Incidentally, this prejudice against Liszt is particularly strongly in evidence in this country. Professor Dent, for example, has said somewhere, quite rightly, that English musicians in general have an aversion from the music of Liszt amounting almost to horror, and adduces in support of his depreciatory estimate of Elgar the fact that he, almost alone among his compatriots, shows traces of his pernicious influence; and certainly nothing is calculated to damage a composer more completely and irretrievably in the eyes of the English musical public than a suspicion that he is infected by the Lisztian contagion. We shall have occasion later to inquire more closely into the reasons for this peculiarly national hostility to Liszt, the violence and intensity of which is always a source of bewilderment to foreign musicians, even to those who do not themselves care greatly for his art, and share the general prejudice against it.

Now, it need hardly be said that such hard-and-fast, cut-and-dried, ready-made, preconceived notions as these we have been examining have always a certain basis of justification. It is no doubt perfectly true that, on the whole, the music of Palestrina deserves the encomiums which are lavished upon it by people who have in all probability never heard a note of it, and would care nothing for it if they did; similarly it is undeniable that some at least of the music of Liszt, and certainly most of it that is best known and most frequently performed, thoroughly merits the denigratory epithets set forth above. Liszt's admirers, however, set little store by the greater part of the works by which he is commonly known; in fact they might even agree with the conventional view of him in so far as it is based upon such works as the Pianoforte Concerto No. 1 in E flat, the symphonic poem *Les Préludes*, the étude *La Campanella*, the *Hungarian Rhapsodies*, and *Liebesträume*, which are about all of Liszt that is familiar to the average concert-gier, and all of which are amongst his least successful productions. It is, or should be, a truism to say that a composer should be judged by his best work, but Liszt, up to the present time, has been condemned on account of his worst. It is true that the musical public frequently displays a disconcerting propensity for taking to its heart the least significant productions of a great master; in our time, for example, Elgar first achieved recognition through *Salut d'amour* and *Pomp and Circumstance*, and Sibelius similarly through *Valse triste* and *Finlandia*.

In the course of time, however, their more important works have come to be appreciated at their proper value, but although Liszt has now been dead for nearly fifty years this consummation has not yet taken place with regard to his music; in concert programmes he is still represented by works of the same order as those of Elgar and Sibelius mentioned above. *Les Préludes* is of all his large orchestral works the weakest, *La Campanella* is the least admirable of his studies in pianistic virtuosity, the *Hungarian Rhapsodies*, if hardly deserving the abuse to which they are habitually subjected, are quite unimportant, and the E flat Concerto is admittedly a somewhat vulgar and flashy composition which, moreover, is played far too often. Indeed, the only great and important work of Liszt which is comparatively well known to the ordinary concert-going public is the piano sonata, and the fact that this truly superb work should still elicit from many critical pens, whenever it is performed, the same stale old *clichés* that I quoted at the outset of this essay, provides the best illustration possible of my contention to the effect that the writers of such nonsense are listening to the music—if, indeed, they are listening to it at all, which is perhaps an unduly charitable assumption—with a subconscious prejudice against the composer. To call such music as this ' tinsel ' or ' pinchbeck '—the two favourite words in the anti-Lisztian vocabulary—is a critical aberration of the first magnitude. The piano sonata is pure gold throughout, probably the most outstanding achievement in piano music of the entire nineteenth century.

In this connexion one is inevitably reminded of the famous experiments with dogs recently conducted by Professor Pavlov (whom God preserve!) of Moscow. The eminent Russian scientist, it will be remembered, after having for some time fed his dogs to the accompaniment of bells, made the momentous discovery that after a time copious salivation could be induced in the unfortunate animals by the ringing of a bell alone. This is what is termed a ' conditioned reflex '—a phenomenon to be encountered as frequently in the domain of musical criticism as in that of canine alimentation. The music of Liszt is a case in point: the inferior works which are all that we ordinarily hear of him have so accustomed us to expect the worst from him that his name alone, irrespective of any particular work in question, has come to symbolize all that is basest in musical art.

Whenever, then—and it is very often—one finds any one giving vent to the customary *clichés* concerning the music of Liszt, one can be fairly sure that he is either totally ignorant of Liszt's work as a whole, or else so hidebound with prejudice that his reaction is not to the music itself but only to an associated idea, as with our Pavlovian dogs. As I have already said, they may be applicable to a certain restricted number of his works, which happen unfortunately to be his best-known ones, but that is all. So far, indeed, are they from being true of his work as a whole that the exact opposite is very much nearer the truth, namely, that a chronological survey of his entire output reveals a steady and consistent diminution in brilliant externality, ending in a bareness and austerity of utterance almost without parallel in music. Moreover, even in many of those works which may seem to merit the opprobrious epithets habitually cast at them, the faults lie entirely on the surface and do not affect the sound core of the music.

In this respect there is a very close relation between the artist and the man. In the earlier part of his career in particular, with all his splendour, brilliance, and generosity, one feels a certain element of ostentation and display in his character which are not entirely sympathetic, suggesting the artistic equivalent of a *nouveau riche*—he is altogether too conscious of his genius. Underneath this slightly vulgar exterior, however, there lay always the fineness and nobility of character which, in his maturity and old age, have perforce been recognized even by those who were, and are, most hostile to his art. In this connexion there is an interesting and instructive anecdote told by his friend Legouvé, to the effect that on one occasion when Liszt was posing for his portrait to the French painter Ary Scheffer, the latter said to him rudely, ' Don't put on the airs of a man of genius with me; you know well enough that I am not impressed by it '. ' You are perfectly right, my dear friend ', replied Liszt quietly, ' but you must try to forgive me; you cannot realize how it spoils one to have been an infant prodigy '. The reply shows all the greatness and fineness of sensibility which underlay the superficial pose involuntarily, unconsciously assumed, out of sheer force of habit and upbringing. Precisely the same phenomenon is to be observed in his art; the element of vulgarity and display in it which has always aroused such violent critical censure is just as superficial and skin-deep as it is with the man, and if his critics had reproached him with it to his face he would no doubt have replied to them as he replied to Ary Scheffer, saying that it was the inevitable outcome of having begun his artistic career as a pianoforte virtuoso.

For this reason the music of Liszt constitutes one of the most searching tests of critical acumen that the art presents. The hasty and superficial critic fails to penetrate through the frequently meretricious outer shell to the solid worth beneath, and only the most experienced and discerning assayer is able to determine correctly the proportion of pure metal to base in the complex alloys which many of his works are. Some of them, again, are admittedly mere pinchbeck, as I have already said; others again, however, are pure gold throughout.

The chief reason, in fact, why critical opinion generally goes so completely astray over Liszt, particularly in this country, is to be found in a definite *parti pris* against brilliance and virtuosity as such. In the same way that we are reluctant to believe that a painted, powdered, and bedizened damsel can be as ' good ' as her plain, homely, and unadorned sister, so we find it difficult to admit

81

that the brilliant and magnificent piano sonata of Liszt, for example, could be as good as a drab and dingy one of Schumann or Brahms. It is at bottom a Puritanical prejudice; at least one certainly finds it most highly developed in those countries where Protestantism is strongest and most firmly established, in Northern and Teutonic countries chiefly. The Southern, Latin attitude is very different; the Roman Catholic Church, of which Liszt was a loyal son, teaches that magnificence and splendour are positive and desirable qualities. See, for example, the *Summa Theologica* of Saint Thomas Aquinas, Part II, qq. cxxxiv, ' Of Magnificence '.

Even if one were to admit, however, for the sake of argument, that the brilliance and glitter of much of Liszt's music are intrinsically condemnable, the stricture only applies to a part of his work. For in the same way that Liszt began his career as a triumphant and opulent virtuoso and then gradually and progressively withdrew himself from the world until he finally took holy orders and died in poverty: so his work, viewed as a whole, exhibits precisely the same steady, unbroken process of recession from all that is superficial, decorative, external, until in the writings of his last years he arrives, as I have already said, at a bareness and austerity of utterance which have no parallel in music. Needless to say, these later works are entirely unknown to those who prate so glibly of Liszt's flashiness and so forth. Not that I would necessarily suggest that they are his most important compositions, any more than that his assumption of holy orders was the consummation of his earthly life. On the contrary, it is probable that the devout churchman in Liszt damaged and grew at the expense of the artist, and that the asceticism of the later works denotes a similar weakening and impoverishment of the genius exhibited in some of his earlier works. The fact remains that to ignore this process of development and its ultimate phase is to misunderstand Liszt entirely; to speak of him as an artist exclusively preoccupied with effects of superficial brilliance and showiness is as if one were to represent St. Augustine as the Don Juan of antiquity and St. Francis as the Casanova of the Middle Ages, simply because they lived loose and worldly lives in their youth. Again, it may well be true that the Tolstoy of *Anna Karenina* and *War and Peace* is a greater artist than the pietistic Tolstoy of the naïve and simple peasant tales with which he occupied his closing years, but to ignore the process of spiritual development which led to this is to miss the whole meaning and significance of his career. Similarly, to concentrate almost exclusively on the early Liszt, or even the Liszt of complete maturity, and to ignore the latest works: to dwell at length on his dazzling triumphs as a virtuoso in his youth and to forget the twilight of his closing years and his tragic end, neglected and penniless, at Bayreuth of all places—this is to misunderstand him altogether. That the composer who, of all composers that have ever lived, has gone farthest in the direction of austerity and asceticism, and finally pushed the modern doctrine of the elimination of non-essentials to such an extreme pitch that he often ended by eliminating essentials as well—that he should invariably be held up to derision and contempt by musical historians and critics and represented as the supreme charlatan and trick showman of music—this is surely the most consummate stroke of ironic perversity in the history of music; for in such works as the symphonic poem *Von der Wiege bis zum Grabe*, the third and last volume of the *Années de Pèlerinage*, the later piano pieces such as *Nuages Gris, Prélude funèbre, Sinistre, La lugubre Gondole*, and others, the last songs such as *J'ai perdu ma force, Sei still, Gebet, Einst, Verlassen, Wir dachten*—in all these works with which he concluded his creative career one finds a quite disconcerting bareness of idiom and a complete sacrifice of every means of effect to the purposes of expression. The conceptions, moreover, to which expression is given in these later works are almost invariably of a gloomy and tragic order, and again in this respect also one finds merely the ultimate point of a constantly growing tendency throughout his entire creative activity. The real, fundamental Liszt, indeed, is not the brilliant and facile rhetorician that he is invariably made out to be, delighting principally in grandiose sonorities and triumphant apotheoses; the essence of his art, on the contrary, consists in a sadness, a melancholy, a disillusion, a despair, of a depth and intensity unequalled, perhaps, in all music. No composer has ever ventured farther into that City of Dreadful Night of which the poet Thomson sings; none has expressed with greater poignancy :

> The sense that every struggle brings defeat
>   Because Fate holds no prize to crown success;
> That all the oracles are dumb or cheat
>   Because they have no secret to express;
> That none can pierce the vast black veil uncertain
> Because there is no light beyond the curtain;
>   That all is vanity and nothingness.

This is the essential Liszt. It is here that his true greatness lies, here that he is original, unique, unsurpassed. Too often, however, as a dutiful son of the Church, he felt himself constrained to give the lie to his innermost convictions, of which perhaps he was not himself fully and consciously aware; hence his pompous, triumphant finales which are almost invariably the weakest sections of his works. Hostile criticism, in fact, is fully justified here in a sense; it rightly perceives in such things a certain hollowness, lack of conviction, and seeming insincerity, but errs in diagnosing the cause of them. Too often, indeed, Liszt went a long way towards spoiling his best works through his assumption of a facile and shallow optimism which is in opposition to his real self and stands in flagrant contradiction to what has gone before. The ending of the *Faust* Symphony is a case in point. The work should logically have concluded with the Mephistopheles movement, and I believe I am right in saying that such was the original conception, but scruples of conscience and ethical considerations generally led him to tack on to the end of it a choral epilogue, a kind of ' happy ending ' depicting redemption through womanly love, which not only impairs the profundity and originality of the conception as a whole, but also constitutes a blot upon the otherwise perfect form and musical logic of the work. This fault, however, does not prevent the *Faust* Symphony from being probably, on the whole, his greatest work and one of the highest achievements of the nineteenth century; for the rest, however, his most completely satisfying compositions on a large scale are those in which the sadness and despair which are the core of his thought and feeling are not thus contradicted, such as the symphonic poems *Ce qu'on entend sur la montagne*, *Héroïde funèbre*, *Hamlet*, and the great piano sonata, the closing page of which I never hear without thinking involuntarily of that terrible little sentence of Pascal, ' Le silence éternel de ces espaces infinis m'effraie ', of which it always seems to me to be the perfecty musical embodiment and equivalent. Even the finest of his sacred music is not that wherein he celebrates the glories of the Church militant and triumphant, as in so many grandiose pages of the *Graner Festmesse*, *Die Legende von der heiligen Elisabeth*, and *Christus*, fine works though they are in many ways, but in such things as his deeply moving setting of the thirteenth Psalm, ' How long wilt thou forget me, O Lord? for ever? how long wilt thou hide thy face from me? ' Here again, however, the beauty of the work is somewhat impaired by the exultant conclusion, which does not seem to ring entirely true.

Another widely prevalent misconception regarding the music of Liszt is that, in the words of Dannreuther in his volume on ' The Romantic Period ' in *The Oxford History of Music*, ' he devoted his extraordinary mastery of instrumental technique to the purposes of illustrative expression '. All the symphonic poems, with the exception of *Orpheus*, are, Dannreuther says,

impromptu illustrations, corresponding to some poem, or picture, or group of concepts expressed in words. They are mere sketches arranged in accordance with some poetical plan, extraneous, and more or less alien, to music. . . . From the point of view of musical design, a lax and loose conception of art prevails more or less through all the *Poèmes symphoniques*. . . . In lieu of musical logic and consistency of design, he is content with rhapsodical improvisation. The power of persistence seems wanting. . . . The musical growth is spoilt, the development of the themes is stopped or perverted by some reference to extraneous ideas. Everywhere the programme stands in the way and the materials refuse to coalesce.

The two chief accusations made against Liszt here, namely, a lack of formal cohesion and a reliance on programmatic ideas alien to music, are both absolutely and entirely untrue. Out of the twelve symphonic poems, which are the objects of these strictures, *Hungaria* and *Festklänge* have no programme at all, *Hamlet* has no other than is contained in the title and makes no attempt to illustrate the drama, *Hunnenschlacht* is merely a battle-piece, also with no further indication than the title, *Tasso*, *Mazeppa*, and *Prometheus* are merely variants on the simplest of all possible musical formulas

85

—*Lamento e Trionfo*—the alleged programmes of *Les Préludes* and the *Héroïde funèbre* are the vaguest kind of romantic *schwärmerei* and contain no concrete images susceptible of illustration, and *Orpheus* is specifically exempted by Dannreuther himself from the strictures above quoted. Only two out of the twelve can be truly said to be programme music in the strict sense of the words, namely the first and last, *Ce qu'on entend sur la montagne* and *Die Ideale*, to which may also be added the *Dante* Symphony, which is only a gigantic symphonic poem in two movements. The first of these is based upon a poem of Victor Hugo which it no doubt follows closely enough in general outline, but the poem itself is nothing more or less than a preliminary sketch for a musical composition, as the few lines which follow clearly show:

> Ce fut d'abord un bruit large, immense, confus,
> Plus vague que le vent dans les arbres touffus,
> Plein d'accords éclatants, de suaves murmures
> Doux comme un chant du soir . . .
> Bientôt je distinguai, confuses et voilées,
> Deux voix dans cette voix l'une à l'autre mêlées,
> L'une venait des mers; chant de gloire! hymne heureux!
> C'était la voix des flots qui se parlaient entre eux;
> L'autre, qui s'élevait de la terre ou nous sommes,
> Etait triste; c'était le murmure des hommes.

This is hardly a programme that can be called ' extraneous and more or less alien to music ', it will be admitted. Rather is it true that Victor Hugo was guilty of writing a poem which is based upon a musical programme that is extraneous and more or less alien to poetry.

In *Die Ideale* the composer follows an entirely different scheme from the poem of Schiller on which it is ostensibly based. The order of the verses inscribed in the score is not that of the poet, but an arbitrary arrangement made by the composer; even then he does not by any means follow the poem line by line, or even verse by verse. Still, it is true that the literary element in *Die Ideale* remains considerable, and without a knowledge of it the work is apt to seem somewhat unintelligible. The same is true of the *Dante* Symphony, but neither of these two works, though they are certainly among Liszt's most ambitious efforts, is among his best. Of them it may be admitted that the musical development is conditioned, and sometimes hindered, to a great extent by extraneous literary ideas, and that the form is, in consequence, loose and unsatisfactory. But to say of the rest of his large orchestral works, as Dannreuther and many others do, that they are completely formless and consist chiefly of ' rhapsodical improvisation ' is entirely untrue, and can, indeed, be proved untrue. This has in fact been done in a recent book written by a German musicologist, Joachim Bergfeld, *Die formale Struktur der symphonischen Dichtungen Franz Liszts*, in which the writer conclusively shows, by means of a most Teutonically painstaking and searching analysis, complete with elaborate diagrams, that the symphonic poems of Liszt are exceedingly carefully, methodically, even pedantically, constructed. How any one can ever have thought otherwise is beyond comprehension. If Liszt is not one of the great masters of form—and he certainly is not—the reason is not that he relies on ' rhapsodical improvisation ' but precisely the opposite, namely, that his form is often, perhaps generally, too mechanical, precise, logical, and symmetrical, lacking in the living, spontaneous, organic quality which is characteristic of the highest achievements in musical form. In some of his best works on a large scale, however, he does attain to formal perfection, notably in the piano sonata, *Hamlet*, and—apart from the slight flaw already indicated—the great *Faust* Symphony, to name only three.

This widely spread delusion concerning the formal looseness and invertebracy of Liszt's major works is, of course, merely another example of Pavlovian caninity. Most of the lesser pianoforte works of his which are generally known have a certain improvisatory quality, and this characteristic has in consequence been unthinkingly applied to his work in other fields, even when it is almost painfully laboured and precise, as Bergfeld shows it to have been very frequently and even generally.

The immense quantity of fine music that Liszt wrote for the piano is almost entirely neglected bp concert pianists, and is in consequence virtually unknown to the general public, apart from a few well-worn and hackneyed show-pieces which are frequently included in the final groups of recital programmes solely in order to display the technical accomplishments of the performer. Many of his best pieces, however, notably in the collections *Années de Pèlerinage* and *Harmonies poétiques et religieuses*, are not exceptionally difficult but, on the contrary, for the most part well within the scope of the ordinarily proficient player, and among the finest in the pianistic repertoire. On the other hand, the difficult *Etudes d'exécution transcendante* are by no means mere virtuoso pieces, but works of intrinsic merit as well, and even many of the greatly abused operatic fantasias are in their way perfect masterpieces. Saint-Saëns has well said that such things are not necessarily any more negligible artistically than overtures, which are generally little more than fantasias on the themes of the opera which is to follow. One might say that, while the overture prepares the listener's mind for the drama which is to come, the Lisztian fantasia is in the nature of an epilogue, a commentary or meditation upon the drama after it is over. The transfiguring imaginative power which Liszt brings to such things is seldom recognized by criticism. An honourable and noteworthy exception is to be found in the writings of a shrewd and penetrating critic of the 'nineties, named George Bernard Shaw. Speaking of the great fantasia on the *Don Juan* of Mozart he says:

When you hear the terrible progressions of the statue's invitation suddenly echoing through the harmonies accompanying Juan's seductive ' Andiam, andiam, mio bene ', you cannot help accepting it as a stroke of genius—that is, if you know your ' *Don Giovanni* ' *au fond*.

Even more remarkable in its critical acumen is his appreciation of the fantasia on Meyerbeer's *Robert le Diable*,

one of those prodigious opera fantasies of Liszt's which few pianists can play and fewer understand. . . . That on ' Robert ' is a pungent criticism of Meyerbeer as well as a *tour de force* of adaptation to the pianoforte. To anyone who knows the opera, and knows the composer thoroughly, no written analysis of ' Robert ' could be half so interesting as this fantasia in which Liszt, whilst vividly reproducing Meyerbeer's cleverly economized and elaborated scraps of fantasy, grace, and power, picks up the separate themes apparently at random, and fits them to one another with a satirical ingenuity which brings out in the most striking way how very limited and mechanical the Meyerbeerian forms were.

Two other neglected aspects of Liszt's phenomenally versatile genius are the few, but superb, works which he wrote for the organ —probably the finest written for the instrument since Bach— namely, the fantasia and fugue on the theme B.A.C.H., the *Evocation in the Sistine Chapel* based upon Mozart's *Ave Verum*, the variations on *Weinen, klagen*, the fantasia and fugue on the choral *Ad nos, ad salutarem undam*; and the fifty or so songs with piano accompaniment, some of which, such as *Kennst du das Land, Es muss ein Wunderbares sein, Kling leise, Ein Fichtenbaum, König im Thule, Vatergruft, Ich möchte hingehn, Ich scheide, Enfant, si j'étais roi*, and many others too numerous to mention here, are among the best songs written since Schubert. Above all, however, does Liszt excel in his settings of Heine, whose combination of sentimentality and irony, of lyricism and cynicism, was particularly congenial and akin to his own temperament.

This strain of irony and cynicism which so often underlies the suave and sentimental exterior of his music is the active aspect of the weariness and disillusionment which we have already noted in much of his best works, and particularly in his later years—the combination of medieval *accidia* and modern *weltschmerz* which we find in his *Hamlet* for example, and in the last songs and piano pieces. There it is passive, despairing, almost resigned; in its more positive manifestations it takes the form of a withering and pitiless mockery of which the most perfect expression is to be found in the third movement of the *Faust* Symphony, the *Mephisto* Waltzes, the *Totentanz*, and other similar essays in the musical *macabre*. It runs like a leitmotiv, however, throughout his entire work; as Busoni says in an essay on Liszt in his book *Von der Einheit der Musik*, ' Für Liszts Ausdrucksvermögen bezeichnend ist die Wiedergabe zweier Gefühlsmomente: des diabolischen und des katholisch-gläubigen '. This, incidentally, helps further to explain the Anglo-Saxon dislike of Liszt to which reference has already been made. The national taste is not sympathetic to Catholicism, and intolerant of Diabolism; not unnaturally, therefore, the combination of the two in one personality is felt to be altogether too much. To oscillate

G

perpetually between the saintly and the satanic, as Liszt does, is ungentlemanly and un-English, to say the least. Similarly, the dazzling brilliance of one part of his work and the intense austerity of the other are alike uncongenial to a race which seeks in all things the *via media*, the happy mean, the compromise between two extremes. This is not necessarily an unworthy ideal, I hasten to add; it has certainly made the British Empire what it is, but it undoubtedly constitutes a formidable barrier to the due appreciation of the art of Liszt for whom, in the words of that regrettably un-English man, William Blake, ' the road of excess leads to the palace of wisdom '.

Whatever one's opinion may be concerning the intrinsic merit, or the reverse, of Liszt's music, there can be no two opinions concerning the immense influence his work has had, for good or evil, and possibly for both, on the history of the art—greater in all probability than that of any other composer who has ever lived. No musician has more generously lavished such superlative interpretative gifts, as pianist, as transcriber, as conductor (during the Weimar period), on his great predecessors and contemporaries; similarly none has more richly endowed his contemporaries and successors with the fruits of his creative activities. Liszt, indeed, quite simply, is the father of modern music. There is no composer of any importance during the latter part of the nineteenth, or the beginning of the twentieth, century who has not been influenced by him in some way or another. The first and most important of all was, of course, Wagner. The Wagnerians have always attempted to minimize and gloze over this debt, but Wagner himself, greatly to his credit, never tried to do so but, on the contrary, openly proclaimed it. See for example the well-known letter written to Liszt in which he says: ' Ich bezeichne dich als Schöpfer meiner jetzigen Stellung. Wenn ich komponiere und instrumentiere denke ich immer nur an dich . . . deine drei letzten Partituren sollen mich wieder zum Musiker weihen für den Beginn meines zweiten Aktes [Siegfried], den dies Studium einleiten soll.' Even before he had come so far it is generally recognized to-day that the immense step forward that Wagner made between *Lohengrin* and *Rheingold* is in large part due to the influence of Liszt.

There is no need even to mention the enormous extent of the debt that is owed to him by the most eminent modern German composers; it speaks for itself. The Richard Strauss of the symphonic poems, for example, could not have existed without Liszt, and the same applies to innumerable others. Even Brahms himself, it is interesting and instructive to note, was influenced by Liszt in his early works such as the first and second piano sonatas, where he adopts the Lisztian device of thematic transformation, and in the clearly poetic elements of the third. In France Saint-Saëns was, of course, one of the most fervent admirers and disciples of Liszt, and one of his most sedulous imitators, César Franck, is no less demonstrably and effectually indebted to him, not merely in his symphonic poems but in all his work, and the so-called impressionists were anticipated by him in many of their most characteristic effects and procedures, sometimes by as much as half a century—see, for example, such things as ' Au bord d'une source ' and the ' Jeux d'eaux à la Villa d'Este ' in the *Années de Pèlerinage*, and the ' Prédication aux Oiseaux ' of the *Légendes*, also the augmented fifths and whole-tone scales encountered in works written as early as the 'thirties. Again, the American critic Huneker has described Liszt, not without justice, in his book on him, as ' the first cosmopolitan in music ', and as such he has a numerous, if somewhat undistinguished, progeny in every country in Europe—the Moskowskis, Glazounovs, Rachmaninovs, Dohnányis, and so forth are all direct descendants of Liszt; equally justly, however, he can be regarded as the first of the nationalists, not merely by virtue of his *Hungarian Rhapsodies* and other similar works, which were practically the first of their kind, but also on account of the encouragement and inspiration he gave to the formation of national schools in many countries. Balakirev, the founder of the Russian nationalist school, and Borodin, to say nothing of Rimsky-Korsakov, were deeply influenced by Liszt; so also were the Bohemian nationalists Smetana and Dvořák, Albeniz, and through him the modern Spanish nationalists, and even the Norwegian Grieg. Other eminent composers possessing no distinctively nationalistic traits or anything else in common who have likewise been deeply influenced by him are Busoni, who is in many respects the very reincarnation of Liszt,

91

Scriabin, whose witch's cauldron contains many ingredients stolen from him, and, as we have already seen, Elgar. Traces of his thought can even be perceived where no direct influence exists. For example, the passage of interlocking common chords of C natural and F sharp in Stravinsky's *Petrouchka*, described in the score as ' Malédictions de Petrouchka ', is basically identical with an episode in the posthumous and only recently published concerto for piano and strings of Liszt, entitled *Malédiction*—a strange and arresting coincidence, this, by the way. Even Arnold Schönberg and the atonalists derive in many respects from Liszt. The perverse and ironic romanticism of *Pierrot Lunaire*, for example, is only a development of that in the amazing third movement of the *Faust* Symphony, and in his last works Liszt clearly foreshadows the principles of atonality. Incidentally, in this connexion it is amusing to note a passage in Dannreuther's volume on the Romantic Period already referred to, in which we are told that even as early as the 'thirties Liszt earnestly worked at the conception of a possible *ordre omnitonique* which might be destined at some distant date to supersede our present tonality. ' It is a fact stranger still ', continues Dannreuther with sublime innocence, ' that Liszt, all his life long, should have retained such a notion, and that he desired to make, and was ever ready to encourage, experiments in tonality which led to effects of interesting ugliness.' Strangest of all, however, is the fact that Liszt's *ordre omnitonique* has to-day become an accomplished reality. Assuredly, that much maligned lady, the Princess Wittgenstein, was not far wrong when she wrote that ' On ne le comprend pas encore—beaucoup moins que Wagner. Liszt a jeté sa lance beaucoup plus loin dans l'avenir. Plusieurs générations passeront avant qu'il soit entièrement compris.' There are many clear indications, however, that the day is at last approaching when Liszt will be recognized as not merely the most potent germinative force in modern music, but also, in his own right, as the inspired creator of some of the greatest and most original masterpieces of the nineteenth century.

1933

Pietro Raimondi

THE WORLD of art, like the world of nature, has its prehistoric monsters, extinct species, freaks and ' sports ' of every kind; music, no less than zoology, can show many queer fauna, aesthetic equivalents to the megalosaurian, the giant panda, the dodo, axolotl, or manatee—some of them comic, some pathetic, some sinister, others positively sublime in their ineffable preposterousness. Of all extinct schools of music that of Naples is probably the most completely dead; of all composers who ever lived there is surely none queerer and stranger than the last of that illustrious line, Pietro Raimondi. To belong to an extinct race and at the same time to be, within that race, a freak or sport—such was the singular destiny of Raimondi. There is, indeed, something mythical and fabulous about him, and it is difficult to believe that he was born as late as 1786, or that he lived on into such comparatively modern times as 1850. He seems to belong to another world altogether.

Like many other people, probably, I had heard vaguely of the existence at some time or other of a composer, who was alleged to have performed the prodigious feats of contrapuntal virtuosity which in fact Raimondi performed; but I had never suspected that the works actually still existed and were accessible, or that their creator had lived in such recent times. It was not until I came across a reference to him in the correspondence of Liszt, quite by chance, that my serious attention was drawn to him. It is contained in a letter written by Liszt to his friend Salvatore Marchesi, dated 12 August 1853.

' As regards great compositions, let us speak of Pietro Raimondi. You are acquainted personally, then, with that extraordinary man whose works by report are such as to cause his actual existence to seem almost problematic.—You know him, I say, and have actually seen him in flesh and blood? Three oratorios which can each be performed separately, and all three simultaneously—Joseph, Potiphar and Jacob. Try to imagine what it must be like! For myself I am astounded and stupefied and ready to proclaim the accomplishment of a miracle. As soon as I had heard of it through the newspapers, about a year ago, I wrote at once to my friend Dehn at Berlin, the superintendent of the musical department of the Royal Library, asking him to make detailed inquiries through the Prussian Embassy at Rome concerning these pyramids of counterpoint which Raimondi has raised up with his own unaided hands. He promised to do so, and in the meanwhile sent me several fugues written by the same composer in sixteen parts of which each can be played separately, or all four simultaneously.' (Liszt is obviously writing hastily—what he means is, a set of four fugues in four parts, each of which, etc.) 'This is already a prodigious combination; but a trinity of oratorios and, more than that, as you tell me, a trinity of operas—one serious, the other comic, and the two capable of being executed and represented at the same time. Jesus —Mary—Joseph! What is one to think of it all! I cannot overcome the amazement which this conception and its realization have aroused in me, and I should be greatly obliged if you would write to Raimondi, saying (1) that I present to him my humble reverence and respects as to the *maestro dei maestri* of the art of counterpoint, (2) that I am infinitely desirous of seeing with my own eyes the three scores of the triple oratorio and of the triple opera. So long as one has not seen and really studied such a marvel, it is difficult to believe in its existence—and besides, it is only after becoming acquainted with it that one is in a position to determine the means of execution which it would require. For it goes without saying that I am not only well disposed but sincerely anxious to do everything possible in order to secure a satisfactory performance of this immense work in Germany, which is the country in which the cultivation of the art of counterpoint is most widely spread. Request of Raimondi, therefore, that he should send me, through the intermediary of the Prussian legation in Rome, his six scores of the operas and oratorios. Moreover, I have learnt from the notice which Fétis has published on Raimondi that he has also made settings of the 150 Psalms. This is also a work in which I am naturally enormously interested, and if Raimondi would be so kind as to add some of these psalms to the other things to be sent, I should be very greatly obliged to him.'

The works mentioned by Liszt in this letter, though doubtless the most prodigious and sensational of Raimondi's compositions, only represent a small part of his colossal output, which comprised no less than sixty-two operas, twenty-one ballets in two and three acts, five oratorios (not counting the triple oratorio mentioned above), four masses with orchestral accompaniment, two masses for double chorus in the strict *a cappella* style, two Requiems with orchestral accompaniment, and another in sixteen strict parts, a Credo for the same number of voices, three settings of the Miserere, three of the Stabat Mater, and three of the Tantum Ergo, for various numbers of voices, two symphonies for large orchestra constructed so as to be played separately or together like the oratorios and operas mentioned in Liszt's letter, innumerable fugues and miscellaneous compositions and, finally, and in some ways perhaps most astonishing of all, a fugue for sixteen choirs in sixty-four parts, a set of four fugues in four parts, in different keys, which can be performed separately or together (this is probably the work mentioned by Liszt above, although he does not mention the different keys), and another similar set of six four-part fugues in different keys, combining into one of twenty-four parts!

Whether Raimondi ever sent his scores to Liszt as requested, or whether the latter ever saw them at all, we do not know. All we do know is that Liszt's enthusiasm waned rapidly, and we find him writing to Moritz Hauptmann in 1855 concerning Raimondi, as follows: ' Along this path there is little to seek and still less to find. The silver *pfennig* in the Dresden *Kunst-Cabinet*, on which ten Lord's Prayers are engraved, has the advantage of relative harmlessness, so far as the public is concerned, over such artistic contrivances as these.' And such has been the verdict of posterity—if, indeed, posterity can be said to have paid any attention to Raimondi at all. After the first outburst of astonishment and admiration in which, as we have seen, Liszt fully shared, complete oblivion seems to have descended on Raimondi apart from the appearance of a short monograph in 1867, entitled *Memorie intorno a Pietro Raimondi*, by F. Cicconetti, and the usual notices to be found in the *Biographie universel des Musiciens* of Fétis, and in Grove's *Dictionary of Music and Musicians*, which latter concludes as follows: ' Such stupendous

95

labours are, as Fétis remarked, enough to give the reader the head-ache; what must they have done to the persevering artist who accomplished them? But they also give one the heartache at the thought of their utter futility. Raimondi's compositions, with all their ingenuity, belong to a past age, and we may safely say that they will never be revived.'

This certainly seems to be a fairly safe prediction. It does not seem likely that any of Raimondi's transcendent feats of contra-puntal virtuosity will ever again be performed—' again ' for, as we shall see, the triple oratorio at least was actually performed in public. He remains, none the less, a fascinating figure, and one who merits far more attention from musical historian, scholars, and critics than he has so far received: on more grounds than one, and for some reasons which could not possibly have presented themselves to Sir George Grove (who was himself responsible for the notice on Raimondi in the publication which bears his name). For example, he appears to be the first composer in the history of music to attempt, deliberately and systematically, to write in two or more keys simultaneously. In other words he is historically considered the father of the modern device known as polytonality. If for no other reason he would surely be worthy of our serious consideration to-day.

Pietro Raimondi was born in Rome on the 20 December 1786, of poor parents. His father died when he was only eleven years of age, and his mother married again in the following year, thereupon abandoning her son to the care of her former sister-in-law, while she departed to Genoa with her new husband. Raimondi was at first intended for the Church, but after two years of study decided that he had not the vocation; he wished to be a musician and nothing less would satisfy him. His aunt consented and took him to Naples, where he studied in the celebrated conservatoire of the Pietà dei Turchini for six years, during which he acquired a complete com-mand of the technique of musical composition as it was taught in those days—and a much more thorough and severe training it was in those days than it is now.

At the end of this period he seems to have fallen out of favour with his hitherto accommodating aunt, who brusquely informed him one day that she had decided henceforth to live in Florence and also that she no longer intended to support him. Not being able to pay any further fees for his tuition at the Pietà dei Turchini, he decided to leave Naples and return to Rome, which he did on foot owing to lack of funds. Eventually in utter penury he made his way to Florence and sought to change his aunt's decision, but she remained obdurate. After a short spell in the hospital at Santa Maria Nuova, where he recovered his health, which had suffered from his severe privations, he decided to appeal for help to his mother. He travelled accordingly, again on foot, to Genoa, and he appears to have been successful in persuading his mother to assist him. At any rate he settled down in Genoa, and shortly after his arrival became known through his first opera, *Le Bizarre d'amore*, which was played there with considerable success in 1807. From that time onwards his future seemed assured, and no year passed without an opera from his pen, commissioned by one or other of the leading opera houses of Italy.

No sooner was he successfully launched on his career, however, than there appeared suddenly on the horizon the dazzling star of Rossini, Raimondi's junior by only six years. The old Neapolitan operatic tradition, of which Raimondi was the legitimate heir and the most gifted living representative, suffered instantaneous eclipse, and the subsequent appearance in rapid succession of Bellini, Donizetti, and Verdi gave the *coup de grâce* to the venerable tradition. Raimondi continued to write for the stage, and by no means without success. In 1824 he became director of music for all the royal theatres of the kingdom of Naples, and in 1831 achieved his greatest triumph with an opera buffa entitled *Il Ventaglio*, which was performed throughout Italy. Altogether, it is interesting to note, he was more successful in comic than in serious opera, like so many masters of the Neapolitan school, such as Leo and Logroscino, for example. Like them again, he combined this talent for *opera buffa* with a complete command of all the resources of the traditional music of the Church. Almost all the greatest masters of the school, indeed, from its founder Alessandro Scarlatti onwards, exhibit this curious duality of excelling equally in the light ribald and gay *genre* and in that of devotional solemnity. In the one they cultivated a

97

style of the utmost simplicity and directness, in the other one of subtlety and intricacy.

Raimondi was in this respect typical of the school to which he belonged, and it is consequently not surprising to find that, defeated in the operatic field by Rossini and his brilliant successors, he should have tended increasingly as time went on to devote his energies to the cultivation of the religious field in which his supremacy could not be challenged. The Dutch scientist Marais, in his fascinating study of the white termite ant, has described how this insect, if its habitation is disturbed, abandons its normal activities and builds a fantastic kind of tower; similarly Raimondi as if in protest against the intrusion into the traditional operatic field of the all-conquering newcomers, resolved to build for himself a towering monument elsewhere, before which his contemporaries would halt in amazement and admiration—a kind of Beckfordian Fonthill Abbey ' folly ' of music.

In 1850, Raimondi became *maestro di cappella* at St. Peter's in Rome, and two years later he produced, after a gestation of exactly nine months, his astonishing triplet oratorios to which allusion was made at the outset. The work was performed in the Teatro Argentina in Rome during the month of August, 1852. On the first evening *Putifar* was played, on the second *Giuseppe*, on the third *Giacobbe*, and on the fourth all three were performed simultaneously by a body of soloists, chorus and ochestra totalling four hundred and thirty. Each oratorio was directed by a different conductor separately, and on the fourth evening by all three, under the direction of a super-conductor in the person of the composer himself.

The effect, we are told, was overwhelming. To quote Fétis: ' When the audience which filled the Teatro Argentina heard the three orchestras, the three choirs, and the three groups of soloists united into a single body of over four hundred musicians in the simultaneous execution of the three works; impressed by the majesty of the *ensemble* in which the details, moreover, retained all their clarity, the audience was deeply moved by the supreme intellectual power which had conceived such effects; the entire house rose spontaneously to its feet, uttering shouts of admiration; an agitation impossible to describe reigned throughout the auditorium, clapping of hands, wild gesticulations, enthusiastic cheers, broke out on all sides, while women, leaning out of the crowded boxes, waved their handkerchiefs. Raimondi had succeeded in containing within himself the consciousness of his powers up to the age of sixty-six; he had learnt to resign himself philosophically to the relative obscurity in which he had remained all these years, but he was unable to endure the emotion caused by the incomparable success which had come to crown his declining years. He fainted, and bystanders were obliged to carry him from the platform, away from the tumult, in order to restore him to consciousness.'

Raimondi did not live to enjoy his triumph for long. Slightly more than a year later, on the 30 October 1853, he died.

The score, which measures no less than five feet by five (!) is in the possession of the Biblioteca Musicale di Santa Cecilia in Rome, where it can be inspected by the curious. The supreme test involved in such a *tour de force* as this, it need hardly be pointed out, consists less in effecting a satisfactory combination of the three works— prodigious though such a feat may be—as in creating in each one separately a level of musical interest sufficiently high to hold the attention of the audience in the earlier stages of the proceedings. In this, Raimondi has been on the whole remarkably successful. I do not suggest that to-day one could listen to each of these three oratorios separately with any great degree of pleasure, but this would apply to most, if not all, of Raimondi's music written in a normal fashion. In the music department of the British Museum Reading Room, for example, there is a vocal score of one of Raimondi's later and more successful operas, *Francesco Donato*, which is no better, and no worse, than the music of any of the three oratorios considered separately. Raimondi, in fact, was not a great composer in the ordinary accepted sense of the word; on this all are agreed. It only remains to be decided whether the combination of three quite good but not exceptional works can amount to anything more than a mediocre result. Most people, I imagine, would follow Liszt and decide that it could not. I am not so sure myself. Admitting that it is not a great work of art in the accepted sense of the word, may it not still be an admirable and praiseworthy achievement of another kind? Do we not, in fact, tend to take too narrow and exclusive a view of the possibilities inherent in the language of musical sounds? The domain of the written word extends so as to include at one end a simple lyric poem and at the other a complex metaphysical or scientific treatise, or a mathematical equation. We do not reproach Kant for being inferior to Shakespeare as a poet, but that is what we are continually doing when it comes to music. Raimondi's triple oratorio is a colossal intellectual achievement; why not let us accept it and admire it as such, instead of suffering heartache, in the company of Sir George Grove, at the thought of its futility? A great intellectual achievement can never be futile; it is an end in itself as much as any work of art.

Personally, the contemplation of this astonishing *tour de force* does not depress me at all; I find the spectacle exhilarating. It is not as if, after all, Raimondi had devoted to its accomplishment powers that would have been better engaged in the production of ' straight ' works of art. His hundred and more works of art show that as an artist pure and simple he was a failure. It is these other works that give me a heartache and seem futile, as does about ninety-nine per cent of all the music that has been and is written in the past and in the present.

The rest of Raimondi's music in fact is no longer of any interest at all, whereas at least these prodigies of intellectual power are unique in the history of music, and I would rather spend a few hours studying them than in listening to the music of any except one or two composers in a generation. These alone matter, and if he does not happen to be one of them, a composer is better engaged in making something fantastic, ingenious, unique, as Raimondi did, instead of turning out second-rate works of art. In art mediocrity is the one unforgivable sin. It is better to be a Don Quixote than a Sancho Panza: and there is certainly something suggestive of the gentle knight of La Mancha about Raimondi which I find endearing and even positively admirable.

To put the matter in a nutshell, I entirely agree with those who would place a great work of art above any triumphs of intellect and ingenuity such as those of Raimondi, but I would sooner have them than mediocre works of art. In music a purely intellectual achievement has its *raison d'être*.

But is it not possible that there is more to Raimondi's work than that? Granting that each of the three oratorios, considered separately, is second-rate, is it not possible that in the combination of the three something comes to life which is not present in each singly? Furthermore, is not the whole conception of the work merely an extension and elaboration on a vast scale of the idea, particularly favoured by the Romantics, of the combination of opposites; as for example, in the *Symphonie Fantastique* of Berlioz, where the lugubrious tones of the *Dies Irae* are combined with the *Ronde du Sabbat*; or in the *Steppes of Central Asia* of Borodin, in which two dissimilar and contrasted themes, one Russian and one Oriental, are presented separately and then combined? What else, indeed, are the concerted numbers of opera than the simultaneous expression of diverse characters, moods, sentiments and thoughts? And is it not possible that in performance the triple work of Raimondi might achieve an effect which cannot be calculated from the cold critical analysis of the separate ingredients on paper? The enthusiasm of the audience at the performance, as described above, would seem to suggest that this was so, in view of the fact that Italian musical audiences are less prone than those of any other country to be moved by demonstrations of pure intellectuality, however impressive.

It certainly does not require much imagination to conceive the possibly remarkable effect of such a combination as, for example, that of the three introductions—that to *Potiphar* consisting in a graceful melody for women's voices only, which is set against the triumphal chant for male voices in *Joseph* and the tender and elegiac chorus of *Jacob*, even if individually they are not particularly striking; or of the succeeding combination of a recitative sung by the wife of Potiphar, in which she denounces the young stranger to her husband, accusing him of trying to seduce her, with the lament of Jacob for the disappearance of his dearly beloved son, while at the same time Joseph gives thanks to Pharaoh for the favours paid to him; or the passage in which Potiphar swears to be revenged on the traitor, while Joseph admits his brothers into his presence, and Jacob mourns the supposed death of his son. Equally striking should be the combination of a flute solo in *Potiphar* with a trumpet solo in *Jacob*, set against a chorus in *Joseph* accompanied by harps. While the two former are in common time, the latter is in triple time and this continues for about 100 bars. Remarkable, too, is the way in which the narration of Pharaoh's dream in the first oratorio is combined with an elaborate recitative in the second, and the prayer of Jacob in the third—and so on.

I can imagine, too, that Raimondi's dual opera—an *opera seria*, ' *Adelasia* ' and an *opera buffa*, ' *I Quattro Rustici* '—might produce a remarkable effect when performed simultaneously on separate parts of the stage, representing adjacent houses, or different floors in the same house. A heartrending tragedy taking place in the one, and a merry farce in the other, might produce strange psychological overtones. A similar experiment, I believe, has been made in the spoken drama, with considerable success. (Actually, however, this work never saw the light, and I do not know where it is to be found. The labour of composition was completed, but Raimondi died before he had time to score it. He left instructions for the completion of the work to his friend, Cavaliere Platania, director of the Conservatorio Musicale at Palermo, but nothing seems to have come of it, so far as I can discover.)

Whatever may be the aesthetic value of Raimondi's astonishing *tour de force*—and only performance could justify a positive opinion —no such issue arises in connexion with the other sensational aspect of Raimondi's compositorial activities, namely, the polytonal fugues. These are, frankly and avowedly, intellectual exercises and nothing else. Raimondi himself describes them as *Opera Scientifica*, and *Nuovo Genere di scientifica Composizione*. No question even of performance arises here; it is abstract, paper music, its only appeal being to the intellect, as with a mathematical equation of Einstein or Lorenz. Not even Bach himself, in the Art of Fugue, has come within measurable distance of the prodigious feats achieved by Raimondi in these works. Bach, of course, is concerned with writing music at the same time that he is demonstrating his contrapuntal virtuosity, which is something of a handicap from which Raimondi is free.

These works, then, have admittedly no aesthetic value whatsoever, but that does not necessarily mean they have no value at all.

As an intellectual achievement they stand among the most remarkable productions of the human spirit in any field of activity. Two of these works are to be found in the British Museum, and can be studied there. The first is entitled *Quattro Fughe in Una, Dissimili nel Modo, Opera Scientifica*, and it contains a preface addressed to the pupils of the Royal Conservatoire of Music in Paris, which runs as follows: ' Young students, the masterpieces of the ancient masters are the sanctuary of musical science and rightly do the names resound in celebrity of Martini, Scarlatti, Leo, Durante, Sala, and many others, whose works are given to you to study as models and as limpid fountains wherein are to be found the doctrines which constitute the true art of counterpoint.

' But human knowledge is subject to progress, and I hope to have confirmed this belief with facts, in the conviction of having contributed a little to the advancement of musical art. Unless I am mistaken I have done this in my *Bassi d'imitazione*, in my *Quattro e Cinque Fughe in Una*, and in a work entitled *Nuovo Genere di scientifica Composizione*, in which are united simultaneously fugues and canons in straightforward and contrary motion.

' I believed that with this I was finished. But after long reflection there was born in me the idea of pressing further forward still, believing that I should attain to the height of my ambitions if I were able to accomplish more daring and audacious enterprises by combining two fugues of four parts each. As a result of by no means effortless studies it seemed to me that I had in the end succeeded, and the penultimate example of my labour is this which I ask you to allow me to present to you, worthy scholars of a Conservatoire which has given birth to so many distinguished masters. It consists of a piece for four choirs in sixteen parts, in four different keys—i.e. the first in G, the second in C, the third in D, and the fourth in E minor. Moreover, these four fugues in four different keys can be performed separately, one at a time, or simultaneously in combination.

' Another work which I shall have pleasure in showing you later consists in a piece for six choirs of four voices each, of which each one sings in a different tonality, i.e. the first in C, the second in D, the third in E minor, the fourth in F, the fifth in G, and the sixth in A minor, and these can similarly be performed separately or all together. Behold then, what for my part I believe myself to have added to the progress of the art; these my inventions have been suggested to me by long and severe studies and by my love for the Animator of my talent. If by any chance these same should prove to have been of some utility, I shall perhaps be urged forward towards still other further enterprises which occupy my thoughts, all the more so if these should win your approval and that of learned and erudite masters.'

The second, and most prodigious, of these contrapuntal inventions of Raimondi to be found in the British Museum is that adumbrated in the foregoing preface, namely, the set of six fugues for four voices in different keys which combine together in a sextuple fugue in twenty-four parts. The threat contained in the concluding sentence of the preface, to the effect that he was meditating still further enterprises of the kind, does not seem to have been realized. It is difficult to believe that it would have been possible even for Raimondi to have gone any further in this direction. Even as it is, one would have difficulty in believing in the existence of such works as these, did they not lie before one, in black and white. Nothing like them has ever been done before or since by any other composer, nor is ever likely to be. They have a place apart in the history of music. In Raimondi, the artistic equivalent of the eccentric descendant of a long aristocratic line, the last of his race, without an heir, the venerable tradition of the Neapolitan school reaches up to the skies in a final paroxysm, and expires.

1940

Vincenzo Bellini

THE PRESTIGE of a universally accepted opinion is so great that it is sometimes exceedingly difficult, even for the most clear-sighted and intelligent critic, to throw off its hypnotic influence and arrive at an independent point of view. Indeed, a very large proportion of our habitual standards of judgement are merely prejudices, so hallowed by tradition and sanctified by constant repetition as to have attained to the august status and dignity of incontrovertible truths. We are all apt to accept them unconsciously, to take them for granted, in the same way that we take it for granted that the earth goes round the sun. In the words of the Bellman in that greatest of all modern epic poems, Lewis Carroll's *Hunting of the Snark*, ' what I tell you three times must be true '; and we have been told so often and for so long that Bellini, together with his companion in crime, Donizetti, represents the nadir of music, that it is virtually impossible to-day to find a musician sufficiently unprejudiced against him to take the trouble even to look at his work, or to listen to it with an open mind and without preconceived ideas concerning it. For it is a curious fact that it is easier for us to be unprejudiced to the extent of detecting faults in a work which we had always been taught to regard as a masterpiece, than to that of finding good qualities or redeeming features in one which we had been previously taught to despise. Why this should be so it is difficult to say; it is true none the less.

This contemptuous attitude towards Bellini, which has now become traditional, was probably first systematically adopted by the Wagnerians, in accordance with their habitual inability to tolerate the existence of any possible rival, however modest and unassuming, to the object of their veneration. That the master himself did not share in this attitude is clearly shown by an article which he once wrote concerning Bellini, in which he expressed the following sentiments: ' How often must it have happened that, after being transported by a French or Italian opera at the theatre, upon coming out we have scouted our emotion with a pitying jest, and, arrived safe home again, have read ourselves a lecture on the danger of giving way to transports. Let us for once drop the jest, let us spare ourselves for once the sermon, and ponder what it was that so enchanted us; we shall then find, especially with Bellini, that it was the limpid melody, the simple, noble, beauteous song. To confess this and believe in it is surely not a sin; it were no sin if before we fell asleep we breathed a prayer that one day Heaven would give German composers such melodies and such a mode of handling song. To make merry over its defects is quite beside the question: had Bellini taken lessons from a German village school-master, presumably he would have learnt to do better; but that he would perhaps have unlearnt his song into the bargain is certainly to be very much feared. Let us therefore leave to this lucky Bellini the cut of his pieces, habitual with all the Italians, his crescendos, *tutti*, and cadenzas that regularly succeed the theme, and all those other mannerisms which so disturb our spleen; they are the stable forms than which the Italians know no other, and by no means so dreadful in many respects. If we would only consider the boundless disorder, the jumble of forms, periods, and modulations, of many a modern German opera-composer, distracting our enjoyment of the single beauties strewn between, we might often heartily wish this frayed-out tangle put in order by that stable Italian form.'

It will be said, no doubt, that this is the utterance of a young and undeveloped mind, and not representative of his mature views; but this not so. It is true, of course, that later, in his theoretical writings, Wagner says many hard things against Bellini, but so he does against all his contemporaries and immediate predecessors, especially those from whom he found it most profitable to steal. One must always distinguish carefully between Wagner's private and public opinions, between his *ex cathedra* utterances and his personal sentiments; and the fact that he always cherished a warm affection for Bellini is shown by the following statement, made in the last years of his life: 'People believe that I hate all the Italian school of music and specially Bellini. No, no, a thousand times no; Bellini is one of my predilections, because his music is strongly felt and intimately bound up with the words. The music which, on the contrary, I abhor, is that which mocks at the libretto and the situations.'

If I have dwelt at length on Wagner's attitude towards the music of Bellini, it is because one might naturally suppose that an art seemingly so remote and opposed to his own would have aroused his antipathy rather than his sympathy. But it would be possible to quote similar tributes on the part of many musicians of the most opposite and divergent tendencies. The sincerest tribute, however, that one composer can possibly pay to another is to write music, whether consciously or not, that clearly reveals his indebtedness to the other. It would be difficult to name any composer who has been paid so many involuntary tributes of this kind, even by those most hostile to his art, as Bellini. I do not think it is an exaggeration to say that no musician has ever exercised a profounder influence on his contemporaries and successors. Consider for a moment what the specific quality is in the music of the nineteenth century which most sharply differentiates it from that of the eighteenth century. It is not so much the change in harmonic idiom or the development of orchestral colour, great though they are, as a new type of melodic writing. This is the primary factor in the transformation; the others are only secondary. Compare, for example, such typically nineteenth-century themes as those of the Liebestod in *Tristan*, or in the Nocturnes of Chopin, with any characteristically Mozartian or even Beethovenian melodies, and the difference will be felt at once. They belong to entirely different worlds. And the composer who first touched this new note, the man who invented this new type of melody, different from everything which had gone before, was Bellini. A few examples will place this beyond dispute.

Ex. 1

Ex. 2

The first of these examples is the seed from which many of Chopin's most beautiful and individual melodies have grown; the second reveals the origin of Liszt's suave and voluptuous cantilenas; the third obviously suggested to Wagner the ending to the Liebestod.

In other words, the note of ecstasy, of passionate lyricism and elegiac melancholy which came into music in the nineteenth century was introduced by Bellini, and by him alone. Bellini is the father of modern melody, and not one of those who most decry him to-day could write as they do on every page if it had not been for him. Even Berlioz, who professed the utmost contempt for Bellini, was compelled to write in his melodic idiom when he wished to give expression in his music to the utmost passion and ardour. The 'Scène d'amour' in his *Romeo and Juliet* is full of the Bellinian spirit, and even the love themes of Strauss's *Salome* and *Elektra* are directly traceable to Bellinian prototypes. One finds the influence at work in the most unlikely places. This, one would imagine, came out of *I Capuletti e Montecchi*:

Ex. 4

etc.

but no; it happens to come from the Trio in A minor for clarinet, violoncello and piano by one Johannes Brahms.

The above examples and allusions being all of a more or less luscious order, it might be supposed that Bellini's only influence on music was of this kind; that consequently he is less to be praised than blamed. From one point of view, undoubtedly, Bellini can legitimately be regarded as a corruptor of music, as Rousseau and Chateaubriand can be regarded as corruptors of literature. This is, in fact, the fashionable point of view to-day, the eighteenth-century attitude. But even if we may dislike intensely the personal contribution of Rousseau or Chateaubriand or Lamartine to literature and thought, it is impossible to deny the value of their impersonal influence in the matter of vocabulary and language generally—an influence from which all alike have benefited, even those who are most antagonistic to the individual writers in question; not only

Victor Hugo, but also Flaubert, the Goncourts, and through them all the most typically 'modern' and anti-romantic French writers.

So with Bellini. We are perfectly at liberty to dislike and even to despise the more personal aspect of Bellini's contribution to modern music, and to regret that he made Chopin, Liszt, Wagner, and Strauss possible; but ultimately even Schönberg and Stravinsky can be shown to owe a great deal to him in the matter of melodic idiom.

Yes, it may be answered, that is to a certain extent true. We admit that possibly Bellini may be an historical figure of the greatest importance, what Mr. Newman calls a seminal force, but that is all. He showed the way to other composers of greater talent than himself; all that is significant and vital in his art has been absorbed by them, leaving behind nothing but an empty husk in his actual achievement which is no longer of any interest or value to us to-day. He is of no more intrinsic significance to music than the drone is to the beehive. Once he has fecundated the queen bee his sole function has been fulfilled; let him now, like it, turn inside out and die.

Is this wholly true? I think not. In the first place, beautiful though the melodies of Chopin, Liszt, and Wagner may be, it cannot be denied that they are generally very much shorter-winded than those of Bellini at his best. I would not go so far as to say categorically that they were all incapable of writing melodies as sustained and flowing as those of the Italian master, as Strauss, for example, certainly is; the fact remains that they did not write them. Here at least he remains unexcelled among composers of the nineteenth century, while among those of all time only the very greatest, such as Bach and Beethoven, have shown greater power in this direction.

In the second place, there is a purely personal quality in some of Bellini's melodies which have not become common property. Take, for example, the justly celebrated melody of 'Casta diva', from *Norma*.

Do we not find here a purity of line and a delicacy of sentiment which is lacking in the somewhat overheated music of any of the composers mentioned above? Bellini's work may indeed be a

Ex. 5

pillaged ruin, 'like the pagan temples of ancient Rome which served as a quarry from which later edifices were built, but here is surely a Temple of Vesta which has escaped alike despoilers and the ravages of time. Even if nothing else of his survived, this alone would be sufficient to ensure Bellini's immortality.

Granted then, for the sake of argument, continues our imaginary interlocutor, that Bellini is a great master of a certain type of elegiac melody, even one of the greatest, if you would have it so; but this is not enough in itself. He achieved such heights very seldom, while the bulk of his music is so inferior as to be often merely vulgar and commonplace.

Now, it must be admitted quite frankly that there is a considerable amount of truth in this contention. It must be remembered, however, that a great deal of what seems to us to be trivial and vulgar has only become so in the course of time, through association. Bellini's melodic idioms have passed into common speech and become the stock-in-trade of generations of second- and third-rate opera composers, to say nothing of song and ballad writers. ' Every harlot was a virgin once ', said William Blake, and most of the reproach which we level at Bellini should by rights be directed at those responsible for the corruption and defilement of his once virginal muse. The same process is to be seen at work in the art of every age, our own not excepted; the artist's personal idiom is first employed by a few, then rapidly becomes popular, and is finally vulgarized and debased. The harmonic and melodic idioms of *Tristan*, once considered so abstruse and incomprehensible, are to be heard every day in the cinema; Underground posters and advertisements follow the manner and method of Cézanne, Gauguin and van Gogh.

These considerations must be taken into account when we reproach Bellini with the triviality and vulgarity of a great part of his music. They cannot, however, be said to exonerate him entirely. It is impossible to deny, for example, that the beauty of ' Casta diva ' is greatly impaired by the banality and emptiness of the succeeding section. But even here we must be careful to guard against prejudice. Every generation of composers employs its own particular variety of musical stuffing and padding. In each instance the comparative novelty of the procedure disguises the underlying emptiness, in the eyes of contemporary observers; it is only after it has become familiar, as that of Bellini has to-day, that it seems surprising it should ever have been tolerated. Intrinsically, however, it is no more empty and trivial than Beethoven's interminable scale passages, Wagner's mechanical sequences, the chromatically descending sevenths of Delius, or the endless repetitions of the same bar or two which we encounter in most modern music. There is every reason to suppose that all these procedures will seem as wearisome and banal to the ears of future generations of musicians as those of Bellini do to ours. They will no doubt be endured with an equally bad grace on account of the manifold beauties which they environ and enfold.

Finally, it must always be borne in mind that the sound of such things is often very different from their appearance on paper, or their effect when played on the piano. This fact is readily admitted when orchestral music is in question; it is not generally realized that it applies with even greater force to vocal music. The simplest and most obvious melodic progressions are those which sound best when sung; the complex and elaborate almost invariably fails in its effect. And so with the music of Bellini. What may seem to us to be trivial and colourless melody is often in reality a most delicately constructed organism, demanding a particular *tessitura* and general style of singing of which we have no longer any conception. In consequence of the modern instrumental treatment of the voice, the secret of singing such music is almost entirely lost; except for a few representatives of the older generation, such as Battistini, there is nobody who can render it in the proper manner. It is indeed a curious reflection that, while to-day the greatest virtue a composer can possess is a sense of instrumental values and a supreme talent for orchestral virtuosity, it is considered almost a crime to write effectively for the voice.

But perhaps the commonest reproach which is made against Bellini concerns the bareness and poverty of his harmony and the crudity of his orchestral accompaniments. On the face of it the reproach has a certain justification, but a moment's consideration will show that it also is largely the outcome of our modern prejudices. Can anyone seriously contend that Bellini's music would be improved by enriching his harmonies and providing it with an elaborate instrumental texture? On the contrary, his vocal writing could only be impaired by such treatment. Like folk-song, it instinctively rejects harmonic elaboration as foreign to its nature. On the other hand, unlike folk-song, it demands some kind of background. In the same way that a jewel is displayed to better advantage in a simple setting than in none at all, but overshadowed by the brilliance of an elaborate one, so a melody of Bellini requires a certain degree of accompaniment which must never be allowed to become so obtrusive as to distract our attention from the melody, or to impress itself too strongly on our consciousness. It is interesting to learn that Bizet, who had been commissioned to re-score *Norma*, came eventually to this conclusion, and gave up the task in despair, saying, ' For these melodies the appropriate accompaniment is that given to them by Bellini '; and another composer of very different tendencies, namely, Cherubini, similarly observed, ' It would be impossible to place any other accompaniments underneath these melodies '.

113

The final conclusion to which all these adverse criticisms of Bellini tend is that he possessed considerable natural talent, but was unable to turn it to its best advantage on account of his grave technical deficiencies; that if he had only taken the trouble to learn his *métier* properly he might in time have written good music. All these statements are entirely unfounded. Those of his friends who knew him as a young man all testify to the fact that he worked very diligently at the Naples Conservatoire under Zingarelli; that not content with this, he secretly took lessons with other masters at the same time; that he knew all the works of Pergolesi by heart, and had copied out most of the string quartets of Haydn and Mozart.

This theory of Bellini's incompetence and lack of technical resource is based entirely on prejudice and ignorance. If elegant workmanship and striking harmonic progressions and elaborate concerted numbers are infrequent in his operas the reason is not that he was incapable of them, but simply because he deliberately avoided them as being contrary to his aesthetic purpose. It was his expressed conviction that musical artifices destroyed the dramatic effect. (*Gli artifizi musicali ammazzano l'effetto delle situazioni.*) If his critics would turn to his comparatively unknown opera, *Il Pirata*, written before the composer was clearly conscious of his ideals and direction—i.e. before he had written the works which have been considered to be incompetent, such as *La Sonnambula* or *Norma*—they would discover that Bellini possessed as sound a technique as any composer of his time. See, for example, the delicately wrought quintet ' Parlarti ancor per poco ', which forms the finale to the first act. As far as workmanship is concerned, it is as flawless as a quintet of Mozart.

The truth of the matter is that Bellini was a great innovator; like all innovators or highly personal artists, he has been judged according to a preconceived notion of what he ought, in his critic's eye, to have been doing, instead of what he actually set out to do. Berlioz, Moussorgsky, and in our own day Delius, have had precisely the same criticism to contend against.

Bellini himself was well aware of what he had to expect from his critics. He used to say that, whenever he abandoned himself to the natural and unfettered promptings of his genius, a long and thin spectre, with a yellow face and huge staring eyes, would arise and take shape. It would then approach him, and, gazing fixedly into his eyes with a bitter smile, would contemplate ironically the inspiration in his heart, and cause his fingers to tremble on the keyboard. This spectre was the personification of the spirit of Pedantry, and seemed to say to him: 'Beware! what does it matter to me that you have been able to move the spectators, and to excite them to a frenzy of enthusiasm with your beautiful melodies, with your impassioned accents? For in the end it is I who am to be your judge. Woe to you if you have not succeeded in showing yourself to be a master of counterpoint, if there should happen to be occasional weak and simple harmonies in your accompaniments! Woe to you if you should seem to me to have been more inspired than learned!'

When Bellini said that 'gli artifizi musicali ammazzano l'effetto delle situazioni', he was only anticipating the theories of Wagner. When the latter declared that he admired the music of Bellini because 'It is intimately bound up with the words', he showed a very acute perception of the aesthetic aims of his predecessor, which were, in fact, not so very far removed from his own, despite their difference in method and approach. The method of Bellini is to identify himself momentarily with the actor in the drama, and to sum up the dramatic situation in a single melodic line; Wagner adopts rather the attitude of the chorus in Greek drama, and constructs an elaborate orchestral commentary upon the situation. And it is Wagner himself who wrote once that 'The instantaneous appreciation of a whole dramatic passion is made far easier when with all its allied feelings and emotions that passion is brought by one firm stroke into one clear and striking melody, than when it is patched with a hundred tiny commentaries, with this and that harmonic nuance, the interjection of first one instrument and then another, till at last it is doctored out of sight'.

Bellini's method of work, as described by him in a communication to a friend, is very illuminating. 'Since I have determined to write few works, not more than one a year, I bring to bear on them my utmost powers of invention. Believing as I do that a great part of the success of a work depends on the choice of an interesting

115

subject with a strong contrast of passions, harmonious and deeply-felt verses, and not merely dramatic situations, my first object is to obtain a perfect drama from a good writer. Once the work of the poet has been completed I study attentively the dispositions of the characters, the passions which sway them, and the sentiments which they express. Possessed by the feelings of each of them, I imagine myself for the moment to have become the one who is speaking, and I make an effort to feel like him, and to express myself in his manner. Knowing that music results from the employment of variety of sounds, and that the passions of mankind manifest themselves by means of the utterance of diverse tones, I have reproduced the language of passion in my art through incessant observation.

' Then in the seclusion of my study I begin to declaim the parts of the different characters in the drama with the utmost warmth, observing in the meanwhile the inflexions of my voice, the degree of haste or languor in their delivery—the accent, in short—and the tone of expression which nature gives to the man who is in the throes of emotion; and I find in this way the musical motives and *tempi* best adapted to their communication to others through the medium of sounds.

' I transfer the result to paper, try it over on the piano, and if I feel in it the corresponding emotion I consider myself to have succeeded. If I do not, then I begin again.'

In this way ' Casta diva ' was re-written no fewer than eight times before the composer was satisfied with the result. We are a long way off here from the facile tune-trundling which is the conception entertained by most people of Bellini's music. ' Col mio stile devo vomitare sangue ', he once remarked; and we can well believe it. His aim, it will be seen, is not very different from that of the modern song-writer—very similar indeed to that of Moussorgsky and Debussy, namely, to find the declamation which will preserve exactly the accent and the inner emotion of the words. But while they generally remain satisfied with that achievement, Bellini, in his arias, is only at the beginning of his task. While endeavouring to preserve accent and psychological truth, he then attempts to build both these elements into a faultless melodic line. Small wonder if he should sometimes fail! The wonder is that he should have achieved it so often. When he does, the result is as near perfection as anything in music, as in the following melody from *La Sonnambula*:

Ex. 6

Du'n pen-sier - o   e d'un ac - cen - to   rea non so-no, rea non son, nè il—fui giamma - - i, Ah! se fe - de in me non hai, ah! se fe-de in me___ non ha - i mal rispondi a tanto a mor

To hear this and the succeeding ensemble sung as they ought to be sung, is infallibly to experience one of these rare thrills which convince us at once that we are in the presence of great art.

The majority of Italian operatic composers, such as Cimarosa, Rossini and Mercadante, have little or no feeling for the dramatic situation or the expression of the emotion conveyed by the words. It is related of Mercadante that he once set to music the words *cala il sipario* (the curtain falls), thinking that they were part of the text of the libretto. Bellini, on the contrary, is at his best when the dramatic situation is most intense; where the dramatic or human interest wanes in his operas, the musical interest similarly diminishes. Consequently the weakest parts are always in those places where a composer like Rossini excels—where an opportunity is afforded by the libretto for purely musical development unimpeded by dramatic exigencies. At such moments he simply writes the first thing that enters his head; anything will do. He entirely lacks musical invention, and it is in this dependence upon a dramatic and emotional stimulus that both his virtues and his defects reside.

The spirit which animates this music is profoundly Latin. It is true that it lacks entirely the immense vitality and exuberance that characterize the art of Dante, Ariosto, Manzoni in literature; Michael Angelo, Mantegna, and Signorelli in painting; Rossini, Verdi, and Cimarosa in music; its affinities are rather with the softer and more feminine tradition represented by Petrarch, Tasso, and Leopardi, Botticelli, Perugino and Raphael, by Pergolesi, Paisiello and Piccinni. In spite of its *morbidezza* and romantic sentimentality it nevertheless retains the purity of line which is the hall-mark of all classic art. Above all, the music of Bellini is essentially Sicilian. It is full of the scent of the almond blossom and the orange groves of his native city Catania, and the serene light of its unchanging summer skies. *La Sonnambula* is like an idyll of Theocritus, and *Norma*, with all its imperfections, like the ruined temples of Girgenti, a few lovely columns standing up proudly from a mound of rubble, facing Africa.

To what extent, if any, Bellini owed this Sicilian quality in his music to the employment or imitation of Sicilian folk-song, it is exceedingly difficult to say. A little tune such as the following from *La Sonnambula* has obviously many of the characteristics of the songs which the Sicilian peasant sings to-day:

Ex. 7

etc.

but the interactions of folk- and art-music are so complex and obscure that it is quite probable that these melodic idioms were invented by Bellini and imitated from him by the common people. On the other hand, the frequent recurrence in Bellini's music of 12-8 rhythms, called in seventeenth- and eighteenth-century music *Siciliani*, seems always to have been a feature of the popular music of his countrymen. We shall probably be safe in assuming that the influence was reciprocal; that Bellini borrowed a certain amount from Sicilian folk-song, and that it in turn was modified by his music. We are certainly told by one of his biographers that he made a collection of folk-songs when he was a young man, but we are not told whether he made use of it in his compositions.

We often speak of the premature death of great artists and all that has been lost thereby, without taking into consideration the question whether the particular talent was susceptible of further development or not. It is, of course, impossible to dogmatize upon the point, but as a rule it will be found that those artists who have died young have come to maturity earlier than those for whom a long life was in store. Without going so far as to suggest that there is a divine and omniscient purpose at the back of it, one does nevertheless feel that there is generally a definite correspondence between the growth of the artist's mind to maturity and the span of his mortal existence. For example, it is difficult to believe that Mozart or Schubert would have achieved anything more than they actually did even if they had each lived to be a hundred, except, of course, in actual quantity. The former had reached as near perfection as is permitted to mortals, while the latter seems to have lacked just that absolute quality of supreme genius which would have enabled him to achieve any more than he actually did.

With Bellini, on the other hand, one can safely say that it is impossible to estimate what the world lost through his premature death. Right up to the end one can discern a steady progress in every direction which must inevitably have continued for many years. He seems to be one of the few eminent figures in art who have died before reaching complete maturity and relative perfection. In his early years his taste was admittedly uncertain, but in later years he became increasingly self-critical, without the corresponding diminution in creative power which so often accompanies such a development. Although his last opera, *I Puritani*, is perhaps not his best, it is certainly a better whole than any of his others. It has not the same stylistic inequalities, and the general level of inspiration is probably higher, although never rising to quite the same heights as the best things in *Norma* or *La Sonnambula*. In no sense can it be considered to indicate a falling-off, or even an arrested development. If it could be said with comparative certainty of any artist that he died with his work only half done, it could be said of Bellini. We have not even the consolation of knowing that it has since been carried to completion by any successor. It was along the path which he traced out that the autonomous development of Italian opera lay, and not along that which has led to-day to the corruption of its intrinsic nature through its subjection to the baneful Wagnerian influence. His solution of the eternal operatic problem, by avoiding on the one side the pitfall of non-dramatic music-making into which so many of his contemporaries and predecessors had fallen, and that of the anti-lyrical Teutonic ideal on the other, was one of the most wholly satisfying which has yet been made, from a purely abstract point of view. The manifest imperfections of his operas are the result of his immaturity, not of his aesthetic principles, which were fundamentally sound and in accordance with the unalterable nature and the highest traditions of Italian art. The neglect of them has led modern Italian music into a morass from which it will probably never extricate itself.

1922

The Problem of Mozart's Requiem

A WHOLE LITERATURE has grown out of the strange circumstances surrounding the composition of Mozart's Requiem. The basic facts are as follows.

A short time before Mozart paid a visit to Prague in order to produce his opera *La Clemenza di Tito*, which he had composed on commission for the coronation of the Emperor Leopold in 1791, he was called on by an anonymous stranger—tall, gaunt, of sombre countenance, and clad in austere grey habiliments—who inquired whether Mozart would be willing to write a Requiem, and, if so, on what terms and within what period. On due consideration Mozart replied that he was willing to write such a work for fifty (some authorities say a hundred) ducats, but that he was unable to specify an exact date by which he could guarantee completion.

The mysterious visitor then departed, but returned a short time afterwards, bringing with him the sum demanded, and in addition the promise of a further gratuitous payment on delivery of the manuscript, as an incentive to its early completion. No conditions were made as to the style or nature of the composition. He was to be given an entirely free hand, on condition that he would not make any attempt to discover the identity of the individual who had commissioned the work.

Mozart accepted these conditions, but owing to pressure of other work did not at once set himself to the execution of the commission. On his departure for Prague for the performance of *La Clemenza di Tito*, the mysterious stranger suddenly reappeared, as Mozart was about to step into his carriage, and asked, ' What about the Requiem? '. Mozart, somewhat taken aback, explained that his journey was unavoidable, but promised that on his return from Prague he would set himself to work on it immediately, before doing anything else—whereupon the stranger departed.

In the middle of September, 1791, Mozart returned to Vienna from Prague, and, as he had promised, at once started work on the Requiem. Apart from a short interruption in order to complete

Die Zauberflöte which, however, was practically finished, Mozart devoted his entire energies to the Requiem. The mysterious circumstances surrounding the commission gradually took a firm hold upon his imagination and eventually became an obsession. An indication of this is to be found in a letter supposed to have been written to Lorenzo da Ponte, in Italian, in September, 1791.

'My head is distracted—I cannot banish from my eyes the image of that stranger. I see him continually; he begs me, solicits me, then impatiently asks me for the work. I continue because composition fatigues me less than repose. Moreover, I have nothing more to fear. I know from what I feel that the hour is striking. I am on the point of expiring; I have finished before I could enjoy my talent. Yet life is so beautiful, my career opened so auspiciously—but fate is not to be changed. None can measure his own days; we must be resigned, for it will be as Providence pleases. I thus finish my funeral song, which I must not leave incomplete.'

The authenticity of this letter, it should be said, has sometimes been doubted, and it has been excluded by Miss Emily Anderson from her monumental edition of Mozart's letters on the grounds, firstly, that no autograph of the letter has been found; and, secondly, because its mood of gloom and depression stand in contradiction to the otherwise cheerful tone of the rest of his correspondence during this period. The absence of the autograph can perhaps justify suspicion, it may be admitted, but that is rather a negative ground for rejection of authenticity. On the other hand, it is surely going too far to reject it merely because its mood does not tally with that of other letters written during the same period. Most great artists, to say nothing of ordinary human beings, are of a mercurial disposition and are capable of changing mood completely within five minutes, and there is no reason to suppose that Mozart was an exception to this rule. Miss Anderson would seem to suggest that he was incapable of changing his mood even once within a period of several months—which seems an odd thesis. But what seems more important than the absence of the autograph or the alleged discrepancy of mood is the internal evidence: the letter seems somehow to ring true, and it is accepted as genuine by Schiedermair, the German editor of Mozart's letters. What is more important still is the fact that the mood of the letter is reflected in the Requiem itself.

However that may be, there can be no question but that the strange circumstances of the commission worked upon Mozart's imagination until he came almost to believe that his mysterious visitant was a supernatural agent, like the Stone Guest in his own *Don Giovanni*, and that he had in fact been commissioned to write the Requiem for his own death.

As his health grew gradually worse, so the obsession increased. Believing that his work on the Requiem was responsible to some degree for his ill-health, Mozart's wife, Constanze, persuaded him to put it aside for a time, and as a consequence his health improved. No sooner was he better, however, that he started work on it again, and quickly relapsed into his former dejected condition of both mind and body. He became gradually weaker, took to his bed, and never rose from it again. Even on his death-bed he continued feverishly to work at it, and even on the very day of his death he insisted on singing through parts of it with several friends. During the performance of the first bars of the *Lacrimosa* Mozart began to weep bitterly and laid the score aside. Later in the day he called his pupil Süssmayer to his bedside—this is important—and earnestly discussed the Requiem with him. He then gradually became weaker and died a few hours later, his thoughts occupied with the Requiem up to the very last conscious moment.

After Mozart's death his widow's first thought was for the Requiem, and not without good reason. She was left almost penniless, with a family of small children, and in addition, it must be remembered, the Requiem had been paid for in advance. As the score remained unfinished, Constanze was not unnaturally afraid that she would be called upon to refund the sum already paid for it. Accordingly, she conceived the idea of having the work completed by some other hand and passing off the whole work as an authentic finished work of Mozart. Several musicians were approached and eventually one Eybler, chief of the court orchestra at Vienna, consented to undertake the work under a strict bond of secrecy. After a short time, however, he became dissatisfied with his work and gave it up. Eventually the task was offered to Süss-mayer, who carried it through successfully. His score, incidentally, was in a handwriting so similar to that of Mozart that no one at the time was able to find any difference between them.

For his part in the deception Süssmayer has been violently abused by priggish and puritanical critics. It is difficult to see why. His only motive seems to have been the generous and disinterested one of helping the widow of his friend and master in a moment of acute financial embarrassment. He does not appear to have derived any profit from what must have been an arduous and thankless task. He probably thought that, once the score had been handed over to the purchaser, nothing more would be heard of the matter, and Constanze's credit would be saved. The repercussions of the innocent (so far as he was concerned) deception were due to the avarice and cupidity of Constanze. Not content with delivering over the score to the purchaser, she kept a copy of it for herself, which she proceeded to perform and have published as if it were her property and not that of the mysterious stranger, to whose real identity we must now turn our attention.

In the village of Stuppach, Lower Austria, not far from Vienna, there lived a wealthy landowner, by name Count von Walsegg. A great music-lover, maintaining several musicians in his service, and an executant on both violin and flute, he also cherished ambi-tions to be regarded as a composer; in pursuance of which design he would frequently commission works from eminent contemporary masters which he laboriously copied out in his own handwriting and presented to the world as his own creations.

In 1791 his wife died, and he conceived the project of doing honour to her memory by commissioning a Requiem which, according to his custom, he intended to pass off as his own com-position. After mature consideration, he decided that Mozart was the most fitting instrument for his designs, and accordingly he dispatched one of his stewards, named Leutgeb, to Vienna, in order to discover whether the composer was favourably inclined towards the acceptance of such a commission. The mysterious supernatural visitant, then—like a figure out of Hoffmann—whose dramatic appearances had so impressed and in the end terrified Mozart, was merely a respectable family retainer in the service of a wealthy amateur musician.

It is not known how Constanze, after the death of the composer, was able both to convince the Count, through his emissary, of the existence of the work in absolute completion, and also at the same time to delay delivery of the manuscript until she had been able to enlist the services of another composer whose task it was to finish the work in such a way as to preclude any suspicion as to its authenticity.

All we know is that she managed to do it, and on receipt of the manuscript Count Walsegg, blissfully unaware of the fact that the composer's widow had retained a copy for her own purposes, set himself to transcribe the entire score in his own hand with the proud superscription of ' Requiem composto dal Conte Walsegg ', which he then had performed as his own work, firstly in Neustadt, near Vienna, and later at his estate on the Sommering. It must, therefore, have come as something of a shock to the Count when he learnt that the work had almost simultaneously been performed in Vienna under the name of Mozart. Not unnaturally, he would seem to have decided that the best course was to say nothing and do nothing. This policy he maintained until the pertinacious Constanze, not content with frequent lucrative performances of the Requiem, sought to have the work published; whereupon he instituted legal proceedings which he was only with difficulty persuaded to abandon, on being given several unpublished manuscripts of Mozart in compensation.

Breitkopf and Härtel, to whom the work had been submitted for publication, were by no means satisfied with the authenticity of the work, and demanded a precise statement on the subject from Constanze. This she gave in the following letter:

' As to the Requiem, it is true that I possess the celebrated one which my husband wrote shortly before his death. I know of no Requiem but this, and declare all others to be spurious. To what extent it is his own composition—it is his until near the end—I shall inform you when you receive it from me. The circumstances were as follows. When he felt his end approaching, he spoke with Herr Süssmayer, the present Imperial Capellmeister, and requested him, if he should die without finishing it, to repeat the first fugue in the last part, as is customary, and told him also, how he should develop the conclusion, of which the principal themes were here and there already indicated in some of the parts—and this Herr Süssmayer actually did.'

Breitkopf and Härtel were not entirely satisfied with this explanation, and on pressing Constanze for further and more precise information, were referred by her to Süssmayer himself. In reply to a request from them for elucidation of the problem, Süssmayer replied as follows:

'Your letter of 24th January (1800) has given me the greatest pleasure, as I gather from it that you set too much store on the estimation of the German public to mislead them by works which ought not to be set down entirely to the account of my late departed friend Mozart. I owe too much to the instruction of this great man to allow a composition, the greater part of which is my work, to be given out for his, as I am firmly convinced that my work is unworthy of this great man. Mozart's composition is so unique and, I venture to assert, so unattainable by the greater part of living composers, that any imitator attempting to pass off his work for that of Mozart, would come off worse than the crow in the fable, who decked himself out in peacock's feathers.

'I shall now explain how it happened that the completion of the Requiem, which is the subject of our correspondence, came to be entrusted to me. Mozart's widow could well foresee that the posthumous works of her husband would be sought after. Death surprised him while he was still working at this Requiem. The completion of the work was, for this reason, offered to several musicians; some of whom could not undertake the work on account of pressing engagements, while others would not compromise themselves by the comparison of their talents with those of Mozart. Eventually the suggestion was made to me, as it was known that, while Mozart was still alive, I had often played and sung through with him the parts he had already set to music, that he had very often talked to me about the development of the work, and had communicated to me the principal features of the instrumentation. I can only hope that I may have succeeded so far that competent critics may here and there find, in what I have done, some trace of his unforgettable teaching.

' To the *Requiem*, with the *Kyrie*, the *Dies Irae*, and the *Domine Jesu*, Mozart has entirely contributed the four vocal parts and the fundamental bass, with the figuring; but he has only here and there made indications for the instrumentation. In the *Dies Irae*, his last verse was *Qua resurget ex favilla*, and his work was the same as in the first pieces. From the verse *Judicandus homo reus* onwards, I have entirely finished the *Dies Irae*. The *Sanctus*, *Benedictus*, and *Agnus Dei*, are entirely my own construction (*ganz neu von mir verfertigt*), but I have taken the liberty, in order to give the work more uniformity, of repeating the fugue of the *Kyrie* to the verse *Cum sanctis*.'

This letter was published by Breitkopf and Härtel in the *Allgemeine Musikalische Zeitung* at the time of their publication of the score of the Requiem, together with comments of their own, throwing a suggestion of doubt on some of his assertions, and adding that ' Süssmayer's known works subject his claim as regards the Requiem to a somewhat severe criticism '.

This latter line of argument is one which has frequently been followed by those who maintain the essentially Mozartian character of the work and reject the sweeping claims made by Süssmayer as regards his part in the composition. Actually, Süssmayer was by no means the negligible nonentity that many have sought to make him out to be. Not only had Mozart a high opinion of him, in witness whereof is the fact that he entrusted to Süssmayer a large share in the composition of the recitatives and the orchestration of *La Clemenza di Tito*, but he was, according to his fellow pupil under Mozart, Seyfried, ' Mozart's inseparable companion '. Seyfried goes on to add that this close personal contact ' imbued him thoroughly with the master's spirit, particularly in his peculiar and novel style of instrumentation. He had assimilated Mozart's individuality so perfectly that many of his works in the serious style are known to me which I should unquestionably hold to be Mozart's work were I not assured of the contrary '.

In the music section of the British Museum Reading-Room, incidentally, there are piano scores of three of Süssmayer's published works, all of which attained a considerable reputation both during his life and for a time after his death; showing clearly that, if he was assuredly no great master, he was a musician of more than average competence. (These are ' Der Spiegel von Arkadien ', ' Soliman II ', and ' Il Noce di Benevento '.) In short, those critics who wish to cast doubts on Süssmayer's claims must find other grounds than that of his alleged incompetence.

The problem, in fact, of the extent to which Süssmayer is responsible for the completed work is an insoluble one. All we know for certain, the only thing that is admitted by both sides to the controversy, is that the work as Mozart left it was unfinished, and that Süssmayer completed it. Whether such completion was his own original work, or whether he was working on sketches left behind by Mozart, or on oral instructions received from the master on his death-bed, are only matters of conjecture and opinion, not of fact.

So far as fact is concerned the position would seem to be as follows. Entirely from the hand of Mozart are the first two movements—the Introit ' Requiem aeternam ', and the ' Kyrie eleison '. The third movement with its six subdivisions—' Dies Irae ', ' Tuba mirum ', ' Rex tremendae majestatis ', ' Recordare ', ' Confutatis ', ' Lacrimosa '—and the fourth, the Offertorium with its two sections—' Domine Jesu ', and ' Hostias '—were left by Mozart in the form of short score, consisting of the voice parts complete with a figured bass accompaniment. The instrumentation was made by Süssmayer, possibly on directions and indications given to him by Mozart. Up to this point all critics and scholars are agreed except with regard to the ' Lacrimosa ' section of the third movement. In the autograph manuscript it only progresses as far as bar 9, and, as we have seen, Süssmayer, in his letter to the publishers Breitkopf and Härtel quoted above, claims to have taken up the work of composition (as opposed to mere orchestration) at that very point. The facts, so far as they are known, therefore, seem to substantiate Süssmayer's claim. A recent investigator, on the other hand, R. Handke, maintains that Mozart finished the ' Lacrimosa ', basing his conclusion on the internal evidence provided by the music itself, and also on the statement of Constanze

Mozart to the effect that this movement was actually sung through when the composer was lying on his death-bed. Handke is further of the opinion that the remaining movements for which Süssmayer claimed authorship—the 'Sanctus', 'Benedictus', and 'Agnus Dei'—were in part at least based upon sketches made by Mozart himself. Against this theory there is the well-known fact that Mozart was never in the habit of making sketches, but invariably completed his works down to the last detail before confiding them to paper. It is, of course, conceivable that for once he may have abandoned the habits of a lifetime and, under the impending menace of death, hastily thrown on to paper his half-formed thoughts in the hope that they might be fully realized by some other hand— but it is inherently improbable.

Altogether one feels that Handke and others who follow him are too prone to credit Mozart, *a priori*, with all that is best in the score; whenever, as they think, a falling-off is to be perceived, they attribute it to the hand of Süssmayer. In itself, of course, the tendency is not unreasonable, although unfair to Süssmayer; against it, however, is the awkward fact that what is unquestionably the weakest moment in the work, the opening of the 'Tuba mirum', is undeniably authentic Mozart.

There remains the possibility that the missing movements, which Süssmayer claimed to have supplied, had been completed by Mozart but not committed to paper; and that he had played them to Süssmayer who had been able to retain in his memory enough to reconstruct them after a fashion—just as, in later times, Glazounov was able to reconstruct the overture to 'Prince Igor' which Borodin had several times played over to him on the piano.

This explanation would solve many problems, including the curious use by Süssmayer in his letter to the publishers of the word *verfertigt* instead of *komponiert*, meaning 'constructed' or 'put together' rather than 'composed'. But all this is mere conjecture, and it is unlikely that the truth will ever now be known.

From a purely aesthetic point of view the problem of the work is not merely that so much that is attributed to Süssmayer should be so beautiful, and so Mozartian in both spirit and style, but also that so much of what is undisputably authentic Mozart should reveal such curious lapses and inequalities, such errors of taste and judgement. For if Süssmayer seems sometimes unaccountably to become a great composer, as in the ' Benedictus ', for example, so Mozart equally unaccountably becomes an inferior composer, in the ' Tuba mirum ', for example.

Such lapses on Mozart's part are no doubt, to some extent at least, to be ascribed to his mortal illness. But there is more to it than that. One feels a certain stylistic discrepancy in the work—a conflict between the rococo style of which Mozart himself was the greatest representative, and the baroque style of an earlier age which in this work he frequently seeks to emulate. Some critics, indeed, have even compared the Requiem to Bach and Handel, and suggested that in it Mozart was influenced by them, but actually a much lesser known master stands closer to the Requiem than either of the two great Germans, namely, Antonio Caldara. Not merely is there a striking affinity between the frequently chromatic polyphony and poignant emotion of the sacred music of Caldara and of the Requiem, but it is an interesting fact that the Italian master spent the greater part of his active creative life in Vienna. Mozart knew little Handel and less Bach (' little Latin and less Greek '), but Caldara was probably, and certainly ought to have been, familiar to him.

But just as, in this work, Mozart seems sometimes to reach back to the style of an earlier age, so in the underlying thought and feeling he seems to reach out towards the future. One feels that in the Requiem Mozart is trying to do something entirely different from anything he had done before, something entirely new. The Requiem, indeed, occupies much the same place in Mozart's output that the last movement of the Choral Symphony occupies in that of Beethoven. There is in both the same sense of strain, the same resultant imperfection, and we find the same sharp division of opinion among the composers' admirers concerning them. For some the Requiem, with all its imperfections, is the ' opus summum viri summi ', to quote the dictum of that devoted Mozartian, J. A. Hiller—the greatest work of the greatest of men; just as many devout Beethovenians regard the last movement of the Ninth as the summit of the later master's achievement. Other equally passionate admirers of both composers positively dislike both the Requiem and the last movement of the Choral.

I have tried to set forth the facts in this strange problem of musical history with complete impersonality and objectivity. If, in conclusion, I may be permitted to express a personal opinion, for what it is worth, I can only say that, speaking as a devout Mozartian, I feel that there is something wrong, somewhere and somehow, with the work; and just as much in these parts of it which are undeniably authentic Mozart, as in those which are suspect Süssmayer.

1939

Antonio Caldara

ONE OF the most serious blemishes in the third edition of Grove's *Dictionary of Music and Musicians* is undoubtedly the omission of any reference to Antonio Caldara. Whether it is to be regarded as intentional or due merely to some unaccountable oversight is difficult to say, but seeing that his name appeared in the previous editions of the work we shall probably be right in assuming the former. In either case, however, it is to be hoped that this defect will be remedied in the next edition, for although his admirable aria ' Come raggio del Sol ' may be the only specimen of his art that has capriciously survived up to the present day in our concert programmes, Caldara is by no means an obscure or unknown composer. On the contrary, his best work, and notably that of it written for the Church, has always received the respectful attention it deserves from all students of the age in which he lived. Indeed, there can be little doubt in the mind of anyone who is acquainted, however superficially, with Caldara's music, that he is one of the most important figures of the period immediately preceding Bach and Handel, and one of the greatest, if not the very greatest, of the Italian masters at the end of the seventeenth and the beginning of the eighteenth centuries.

Of his life we know extremely little, and what we do know is not of great interest. He was born at Venice in 1670, and became a pupil of Legrenzi, one of the leading composers and teachers of the day. His first opera was produced in his native city with great success at the early age of eighteen, and the next thirty years or so of his life were spent in various Italian cities—Rome, Milan, Mantua, Bologna, etc.—in the course of which he acquired a great reputation both as a 'cellist, in which capacity he was reckoned among the foremost virtuosi of his day, and as a composer of operas and chamber music. In 1712 we find him at Vienna, in 1715 at Madrid, and finally at Vienna again, where he occupied the post of vice-chapelmaster under the celebrated contrapuntist Fux to the Emperor Charles VI, a post which he continued to occupy until his death, in 1736.

The greater part of his work is equally unknown to us, and like that of so many other composers of the period lies scattered in manuscript in various libraries and private collections throughout the whole of Europe. Consequently, to become acquainted with his entire output, comprising over seventy operas, thirty oratorios, thirty Masses, both *a cappella* and instrumentally accompanied, to say nothing of a vast quantity of chamber music and miscellaneous compositions for Church purposes, would in itself be the task of a lifetime. According to the most recent edition of Riemann's *Musik-Lexikon* (1922), a German musicologist, Herr Felix von Kraus, is actually engaged on the task, but up to the present time, so far as I am aware, his promised monograph has not yet appeared.

In default, therefore, of the data provided by a reliable, first-hand examination of the existing works in manuscript, we are compelled to rely exclusively upon the meagre fare afforded by such of Caldara's works as were published in his lifetime, and those that have been reprinted in modern editions. The first category would seem to consist of merely twenty-four Sonatas for two violins and bass (1700–1701), and a collection of two- and three-voice Motets with *basso continuo* (1715), to which may be added a book of Masses with instrumental accompaniment published shortly after his death. Modern reprints, apart from innumerable arrangements of the aria already mentioned (' Come raggio del Sol '), are practically confined to the invaluable large volume of his Church music published in the series ' Denkmäler der Tonkunst in Osterreich ' (XIII Jahr-gang, Erster Teil), by Eusebius Mandyczewsky in 1906, a fine Fugue for accompanied voices in the ' Auswahl vorzüglicher Musik-Werke ' (No. 41), and two specimens of his chamber music contained in Riemann's ' Collegium Musicum ' (No. 44), and in the same editor's ' Musikgeschichte in Beispielen '.

This may perhaps seem to be too small an amount of material on which to base even so modest and unpretentious a study as this of the work of such an exceptionally prolific composer as Caldara. It may legitimately be questioned, however, whether it is ever really necessary to know all, or even most of, any man's work in order to form a reliable estimate of his talent.

We do not need to wade conscientiously through the complete

works of a Beethoven or a Schubert in order to appreciate their greatness or the nature of their intrinsic qualities. In each case a few selected works will serve just as well—perhaps even better, when we consider the vast amount of inferior stuff that each turned out which would be better forgotten—and the same applies with even greater cogency to lesser men. In the second place, it must be remembered that it is a characteristic of the age in which Caldara lived that composers, in contra-distinction to those mentioned above, maintained a remarkably consistent level of accomplishment, and that not until the second part of the eighteenth century, generally speaking (there may be a few exceptions), do we find a wide gulf separating the best of a man's work from his worst. Consequently, even if we had the entire output of Caldara at our disposal, it is improbable that the final impression we would receive of his talent would differ appreciably from that based upon a mere handful of compositions chosen more or less at random. It is true that what we have of it does not enable us to form any idea concerning his merits as a composer of operas, but seeing that there is general agreement among those who have most closely studied his music to the effect that he is first and foremost a composer of Church music, this deficiency need not trouble us overmuch. Certainly what we know of his chamber music—and that is a good deal—bears out this contention, for admirable though many of his trio sonatas may be, they cannot be said to equal the finest chamber works of such predecessors and contemporaries as Corelli, Veracini, Locatelli, or Vivaldi. In what we know of his Church music, on the other hand, he can stand comparison with any composer of his age. The ' Denkmäler ' volume of his Church music may therefore be said to supply us with sufficient material to enable us to form at least a rough idea of the general characteristics of his art, and to serve as the basis for a comparison between him and his most eminent contemporaries in respect of stature and significance.

In his erudite introduction to the volume in question, Mandyczewski justly praises Caldara for his superb melodies, ' of which the noble, soaring lines, the architectural construction, and the deep expressiveness of the words, stamp them as belonging to the finest of a period exceptionally rich in melody '. That this is not excessive praise can be readily ascertained by anyone willing to take the trouble of looking at the works for himself; to give sufficient quotations in justification of this contention would require more space than can be here afforded, for it is not a question of an outstanding phrase here and there, which could be easily detached from its context like an epigram, but of a consistent, homogeneous melodic flow from first bar to last of each composition.

Mandyczewski goes on to say that the rhythmic and harmonic interest of Caldara's work is, on the contrary, comparatively small. The first part of this statement is probably justified; nowhere in his work do we find the rhythmic vitality and inventiveness of some of his compatriots such as Vivaldi or Marcello. This deficiency, however, is to a great extent only the outcome of his qualities, for a high degree of rhythmic interest is incompatible with the particular vein of mysticism and introspection which is characteristic of all his best work, in this selection at least. This quality, incidentally, distinguishes him sharply from all his Italian colleagues, save occasionally Lotti, and might perhaps be accounted for by his long residence in Vienna, and his consequent absorption to a certain extent of Teutonic characteristics. On the other hand, it must be remembered that at this time Vienna was the reverse of Teutonic in its culture and artistic ideals, and we shall consequently be safer in assuming that this striking feature of Caldara's work is essentially individual and personal.

That Mandyczewski should, however, find a lack of harmonic interest in Caldara's music is distinctly surprising, to say the least, for it is precisely the strength and audacity of his harmonic writing, and in particular his great mastery of chromatic resource, that strike one most strongly on looking at his work for the first time. Not that he is exceptional in this respect; indeed, the best Italian masters of the period are often extremely interesting harmonically, and not at all the mere insipid melodists they are commonly supposed to be. Caldara's chromaticism, however, is peculiarly individual, and not confined simply to the exploitation of the semi-tonally descending —or, less frequently, ascending—bass, which is one of the most popular and fruitful formulas of the period beginning with Purcell (or even earlier) and ending with Bach. He certainly makes use of it to a certain extent, and with great effect, like all his colleagues, but his more highly personal progressions are arrived at very differently, in a more deliberately colouristic manner. Particularly characteristic of his style, for example, is his predilection for the progression from the flattened sixth of the scale to the augmented fourth, generally in the bass part, as in the following extracts:

He is also extremely fond of a chain of unresolved, descending chromatic sevenths, as indicated in the following figured bars:

and a more elaborate and truly magnificent example of the use of the device is to be found at the end of his 'Crucifixus', which is quoted on p. 139 *et seq.*

It would obviously be absurd to suggest that these progressions are in any way unique, or even that they are not to be found frequently enough in the work of other composers of the same period. There is probably no single harmonic progression in the whole of music, any more than there is an isolated melodic phrase or rhythmical formula, that has never been used save by one man alone—or if there is it is fairly safe to say that it must be a very bad one. The fact remains that the habitual and consistent employment of such progressions as those quoted above, and the highly personal way in which they are handled, impart a curiously poignant expressiveness and a particular shade of mystical intensity to Caldara's work that one does not easily find elsewhere.

Nevertheless, despite the great beauty of his melody and the power and individuality of his harmony, it is probably his ability to reconcile the claims of both these elements with the exigencies of an intricate and finely-wrought polyphonic texture that constitutes Caldara's chief title to lasting fame. In this respect his ' Crucifixus ' in sixteen real parts is one of the most remarkable works ever written. For it is not as if, like practically all other contrapuntal feats in a large number of parts, it was a mere exhibition of barren mathematical ingenuity, consisting almost entirely of a perpetual oscillation between tonic and dominant harmonies, and entirely devoid of musical interest of any kind. On the contrary, it is a work of intrinsic beauty, all technical considerations apart, and it is difficult to say which to admire the most: the beauty and expressiveness of the themes, the superb harmonic structure, or the consummate ease and mastery with which he handles such a vast number of voices. It is only at the cadences (where it is obviously unavoidable) that any strain or artificiality in the movement of the individual parts makes itself felt; otherwise they progress as naturally, logically, and inevitably as if there were only four or five of them to consider. The stupendous nature of such an achievement from the technical point of view can perhaps be fully appreciated only by those who retain painful recollections of their efforts in student days to write strict scholastic counterpoint in even such a comparatively small number of parts as seven or eight. For Caldara takes no liberties with the strict style save for the employment of hidden fifths or octaves, and consecutives by contrary motion. (Two parts moving from a unison to an octave, for example, or vice versa.) The concluding bars of this superb composition are reprinted on the pages following this essay. It is given in full score, as, owing to the continual and intricate crossing of parts, its linear beauty can be properly appreciated only when thus set forth.

Although his fine Te Deum for two four-part choirs and orchestral accompaniment of *clarini*, trumpets, drums, first and second violins, violas, and trombones, shows that he was, on occasions, capable of great brilliance, it will generally be found that Caldara excels in the treatment of rather sombre themes, especially those associated with the Passion. Particularly noteworthy in this respect are the nobly expressive motets ' Laboravi in gemitu meo ' and ' Miserere mei Domine ', for three voices and *basso continuo*, while his ' Stabat Mater ', from which the opening has been quoted above, is a consummate masterpiece from beginning to end, and worthy to be placed among the finest works of the period. The ' Missa Dolorosa ' also, though slightly more florid in style, is scarcely if at all inferior. All things considered, however, it is undoubtedly the great ' Crucifixus ' that represents the highest point to which Caldara attains; a work which, in nobility and grandeur of conception and sheer technical mastery, has few if any parallels in the entire literature of music.

1929

A Note on Giacomo Meyerbeer

PROBABLY NO more dramatic reversal of contemporary opinion is to be found in musical history than is afforded by the case of Meyerbeer. In his lifetime he was not merely the most popular of composers with the general public, but also the greatest living master of music in the eyes of the majority of the *cognoscenti*. By many, indeed, he was acclaimed as the legitimate successor to Beethoven—no less; and among his most fervent admirers were not merely such literary men as Heine, who compared him to Goethe, and Balzac, who in his story *Gambara*, has painted a portrait of him which is intended to represent the ideal composer—but also musicians themselves, such as Weber, Berlioz, and even Wagner himself who in 1842 wrote a glowing eulogy of Meyerbeer in which he compares the latter's achievement to that of Handel, Gluck, Mozart and Beethoven. (It is true that he thought and wrote differently in later years, but it would be difficult to say which of the attitudes was the more convinced or sincere —that of the enthusiastic disciple or the unsuccessful rival.)

To-day, on the contrary, of all eminent names in the history of music, that of Meyerbeer is probably the one which arouses most contempt and derision, and the least sympathy, whether from the left, right, or centre parties of musical opinion. Whereas other composers may have equally strenuous detractors, they at least have also their passionate adherents; Meyerbeer alone would seem to have none. No one to-day has a good word to say for him. The familiar swing of the critical pendulum from admiration to aversion, or vice versa, has been so violent in the case of Meyerbeer that it has got jammed, and has never swung back again. That he was assuredly not the great master he appeared to be in the eyes of his dazzled contemporaries may be admitted, but is it so certain that he was the contemptible charlatan and time-server that he is represented to be to-day? Is it likely that many, perhaps most, of the finest minds of that time were completely wrong, whereas every musical newspaper hack of the present day, who has probably never seen or heard one of his operas performed as it should be performed, is necessarily right? One would need to be a singularly naïve believer in the doctrine of evolution, and of the superiority of each successive generation over its predecessor, to believe that.

Certainly no one could be blamed for failing to discover what it was our ancestors found to admire in the music of Meyerbeer, from the melancholy travesty of a performance of *Les Huguenots* which was given at Covent Garden about a dozen years ago. To anyone who knew the score it was unrecognizable. Equally certainly no one can hope to discover it from strumming through a vocal score at the piano. Like all thinkers in terms of the orchestra, Meyerbeer sounds peculiarly inept on the piano, and even more than most. In default of a first-rate performance which, it seems, one can no longer expect, there is nothing for it but to study the full score for oneself, and there are few critics to-day who are willing to give time and take the trouble to do so. I can only say that, when turning over the pages of the full scores of *Robert le Diable* and *Les Huguenots* recently, I was as much struck as I was when I first became acquainted with them, some twenty years ago, with the extraordinary originality and imaginative power of the orchestral writing. Admittedly, in order to appreciate it to the full one has to exercise one's historical sense. One has momentarily to forget all that has come since his day and to place oneself in the position of the student or listener of his time. But when one realizes that the composition of *Robert le Diable* dates from the year of Beethoven's death (1827) it is, I maintain, impossible to deny that Meyerbeer was a great innovator—one of the greatest innovators in the history of music.

The trouble with Meyerbeer is, of course, that as with so many innovators, all that was most fruitful in his discoveries was taken over and developed by his successors for their own purposes. To-day Meyerbeer is only credited with what is left over after generations of composers have sacked and looted his scores and carried off everything of value. Many of those who have done so have been honest enough to admit their debt, such as Berlioz in his treatise on instrumentation and several critical essays, and also Richard Strauss—with whom, incidentally, Meyerbeer has much in common—in his annotations to Berlioz's treatise. Others, such as

Wagner, have not been so honest, and have sought to conceal their debt, but there can be little question that the German critic, Riemann, was right when he said that 'history will point to Meyerbeer's music as one of the most important transition steps to Wagner's art '.

It would take too long if one were to attempt to draw up a summary or inventory of the orchestral devices first exploited by Meyerbeer and adopted by his successors. It will suffice to mention a few outstanding examples: he was the first to employ and recognize the peculiar expressive aptitudes of the bass clarinet and the *cor anglais*, and of certain registers of the bassoon; the first, as Strauss has pointed out, to realize the possibilities of the violas, especially in the lowest register, for expression and fantastic colour; the first to write for the double basses alone (without the 'cellos), as in that striking and imaginative passage cited by Berlioz from the duet in the fourth act of *Les Huguenots*, in which he writes for a rich and subtle combination of *cor anglais*, clarinets and horns over a tremolo for the basses; the first to attempt systematically to obviate the deficiencies of the natural horns by writing for them in two or more keys; the first to practise the various doublings and *divisis* which are now the bread-and-butter of every orchestral composer. On a higher creative level is his dramatic employment of the chorus; he is the first composer to make the crowd articulate in opera. Both in this respect and in his invention of the historico-dramatic tableau he is the father of the Russian operatic composers; for all Moussorgsky's natural genius, *Boris Godounov* could never have been written without the example of *Les Huguenots* before him.

From this historical point of view, then, it is easy to understand the high opinion of Meyerbeer held by his contemporaries. In their eyes, rightly, he was seen to have enriched the expressive possibilities of music to a greater extent than any of his contemporaries with the exception, of course, of Berlioz, who, however, came rather later on the scene and, in any case, himself owed much to Meyerbeer. It was only natural that his immense gifts as an innovator should have blinded them to his equally incontestable faults which are now all we see in him since his innovations and discoveries have become common property.

There is, however, one other aspect of his work which, I venture to suggest, is of interest and importance to us to-day. In opera before his time the balance was all in favour of the voices; in that of Wagner and his successors, in favour of the orchestra. In the operas of Meyerbeer, with all their grave defects and countless trivial pages, one finds a perfect balance between the two elements which it should be the aim of future operatic composers to recapture.

1938

Orazio Vecchi and the Madrigal Drama

ORAZIO VECCHI, one of the most eminent Italian composers of the second half of the sixteenth century, was born at Modena about the year 1550. After taking Holy orders he became canon and eventually archdeacon at Correggio in 1586 and 1591 respectively, and such was the favour and high esteem in which he was held by the ecclesiastical authorities that, together with Ludovico Balbi and Giovanni Gabrieli, the great leader of the Venetian school and one of the greatest masters of the century, he was entrusted with the task of revising and preparing an edition of the Church plain-chant, published by Gardano in 1591. The impression of clerical sanctity, however, which these activities would seem to suggest, is somewhat rudely dispelled by certain incidents in his career which, even taking into consideration the times in which he lived, are difficult to reconcile with his sacred calling. In 1593, it would appear, His Reverence the Archdeacon of Correggio was involved in some obscure street brawl, in the course of which he received a stiletto wound from an unknown hand; and about two years later a similar incident is recorded, resulting more happily this time in the discomfiture of his adversary, who received two wounds in the head from the archidiaconal *mezza spada*, or short sword. On yet another occasion a fantastic scene took place during divine service between Vecchi, who was intoning the chant, and the church organist who was accompanying him. Each of them was under the impression that at a certain moment in the service the other should keep silence, and since neither of them was disposed to give way to the other a kind of musical duel ensued in which Vecchi sang increasingly louder and louder in an effort to dominate the organist, who in his turn attempted to drown the voice of the singer with his instrument, to the horror of the clergy and the amusement of the congregation. Largely, no doubt, in consequence of these and similar exploits he was relieved of his ecclesiastical functions in 1595, but such were his musical gifts and the recognition they had gained for him that he was shortly after appointed to the post of *maestro di cappella* at the cathedral of his native city of Modena, and two years later to that of director and organizer of the Court festivities and diversions as well. In the later years of his life his fame extended over the whole length and breadth of Italy and even penetrated to other countries, until finally he came to be regarded throughout Europe as one of the greatest masters, not merely of his age, but of all time. His death in 1604 at a comparatively early age is attributed to the chagrin occasioned by intrigues against him, which resulted in the post of *maestro di cappella* being taken from him and given to one of his pupils named Geminiano Capilupi. He died leaving a considerable fortune and in addition a fine collection of books and pictures, testifying to a degree of general culture and erudition not ordinarily encountered in a musician.

As a composer he was, like all the masters of his time, exceedingly active in the domain of Church music, and a large number of masses, motets, hymns, lamentations, and so forth, which are still extant, bear ample witness to his eminence in this direction. He was, nevertheless, primarily a secular composer, and several of his madrigals and *canzonette* rank among the finest examples of these forms that we possess. (See, for instance, the charming *Pastorella gratiosella*, an extract from which is printed in the second volume of the *Oxford History of Music*.) His present reputation, however, and the important place that he occupies, or rather should occupy, in musical history, are primarily due to his remarkable experiments in the direction of the madrigal drama, or *commedia armonica* as he himself called it, of which the ' Amfiparnasso ' is the most celebrated and perhaps the best example.

This curious and interesting work, of which modern reprints by Luigi Torchi (in his *Arte Musicale in Italia*) and Robert Eitner (in *Die Oper*) are available, constitutes an attempt to realize in terms of music the old Italian tradition of the *Commedia dell' Arte*, with its stock types, still familiar to us at the present day, of Pantalone, Dottor Graziano, Arlecchino, and the rest. The work is divided into three acts with a prologue, and consists in a series of self-contained, unaccompanied, five-part madrigals, each of which corresponds to a separate scene or episode of the text. The plot itself is slight and, moreover, somewhat difficult to follow, even by

149

those acquainted with the Italian language, on account of the fact that the comic characters in the drama, in accordance with the tradition of the *Commedia dell' Arte*, speak in various dialects— Pantalone in Venetian, Dottor Graziano in Bolognese, Zanni and Pedrolino (who are the equivalents of Arlecchino and Brighella) in Bergamasque, and the swashbuckling Capitan Cardon in Spanish.

In the first scene Pantalone calls to his servant who is in the kitchen, telling him to go and persuade one Hortensia, a courtesan, to come to him. The latter contemptuously and abusively dismisses the messenger, and Pantalone laments the fair one's disdain. The second scene consists in a dialogue between two lovers, Nisa and Lelio, and in the third Pantalone promises the hand of his daughter to Doctor Graziano. The second act begins with a soliloquy on the part of Lucio, a young man in love with Isabella, in which, jealous of the attentions paid by the latter to his rival, Captain Cardon, he proposes to commit suicide by throwing himself over a precipice. The second scene consists in a dialogue between Zanni and the Captain, and the third in another between the latter and Isabella—a supremely comic love scene in which the Captain, enumerating one by one the physical charms of Isabella, asks her to whom each belongs, to which the lady invariably replies: ' To Captain Cardon '. The fourth is a soliloquy by Isabella who, having been told that Lucio, whom she really loves despite her flirtatious conduct with the Spanish gallant, has committed *felo de se*, proposes to follow his example, which she is prevented from doing in the fifth by her maidservant Frulla, who informs her that Lucio is not really dead after all. The third act begins with a scene in which Pantalone discusses with his servant Francatrippa what guests should be invited to his daughter's wedding, and the Doctor enters with a lute, with which he proposes to serenade his betrothed. In the second scene he does so, with a comic madrigal reminding one of the similar efforts of Beckmesser in *Die Meistersinger*. In the third, Francatrippa goes to the Jews in order to pawn something, and finds them celebrating the Sabbath in a grotesque chorus set to Hebrew words. In the fourth Isabella and Lucio are reconciled, and the fifth and last consists in a grand *finale* in which their approaching betrothal is celebrated.

It will be seen that, apart from the slender thread constituted by the love affair of the two principals, there is really no plot at all, and that the work consists in a series of disconnected scenes chosen solely on account of their suitability to picturesque musical treatment. The main interest of the work lies in the quite remarkable power of psychological characterization, both of types and individuals, possessed by the composer, and in his capacity for the graphic delineation of situations in spite of the slender and limited resources at his disposal. In all music there is nothing more richly comic than the Jewish chorus in the third act, or the scene between the amorous Spaniard and the fickle Isabella. At the same time in the more serious episodes we encounter a depth of feeling and an expressiveness equal to those of any music of the time.

Considerable difference of opinion exists among authorities concerning the way in which the work was performed. It was formerly believed that it represented a crude attempt to create a form of comic opera, and that when a single character was speaking, his part was sung by an actor on the stage while the other parts were sung behind the scenes. According to another theory, the actors on the stage spoke their lines while the music was sung behind a curtain. This view gains support from the fact that a disciple and follower of Vecchi, named Adriano Banchieri, also wrote madrigal dramas, and that in the preface to one of them (*Saviezza Giovenile*) he gives a definite description of the way in which he wished his work to be performed. Before the beginning of the performance, he tells us, one of the singers should read aloud the title of the scene, the names of the characters and a brief account of the action. The performance should take place in a room, in one corner of which are placed carpets, chairs, and appropriate scenery, while behind the scene are seats for the chorus, facing the public, and behind them an orchestra of lutes and other instruments which play in unison with their voices. The concealed singers perform their music from the parts, while the actors on the stage synchronize their action with the music and recite the words.

It does not necessarily follow, however, that because Banchieri's *Saviezza Giovenile* was intended to be so performed, that Vecchi's *Amfiparnasso* also was. Indeed, the probabilities are that it was not, for, as Professor Dent has pointed out in his article on Vecchi in *Grove's Dictionary of Music and Musicians*, there is a passage in the prologue which would seem to exclude any possibility of a stage setting:

> '. . . voi sappiat' intanto
> Che questo di cui parlo
> Spettacolo, si mira con la mente
> Dov' entra per l'orecchie, e non per gl' occhi.
> Però silenzio fate,
> E'n vece di vedere, hora ascoltate.'

(You must learn that this spectacle of which I speak is to be seen by the mind, into which it enters through the ears and not through the eyes. Be silent, therefore, and in place of looking, listen.)

If this statement is to be taken absolutely literally, it follows that there could have been no kind of stage representation at all—not even in dumb show, as another theory would have it—and that the work was simply intended to be a kind of dramatic cantata, strikingly analogous, as M. Romain Rolland was the first to point out, to the *Roméo et Juliette* of Berlioz, which likewise consists of a series of detached scenes chosen more or less arbitrarily for the musical possibilities they afford. But an even closer and more modern analogy is to be found in *Le Roi David* of Honegger, for it is more than likely that in Vecchi's work a synopsis of each section of the work was similarly given by a reciter or narrator; or in *Les Noces* of Stravinsky, originally conceived, we are told, as a dramatic cantata rather than as a ballet, in which the action is in large part developed chorally.

Apart, then, from the intrinsic beauty, wit, and verve of Vecchi's work, as fresh now as the day when it was written, it is of great additional importance in that it strikingly anticipates by more than three centuries several interesting developments in the music of to-day, and may quite possibly inspire many more in the future.

1928

The Verdi Revival

MR. G. K. CHESTERTON, in *The Resurrection of Rome*, gives an amusing description of the conception of history which, he says, prevailed during the latter half of the nineteenth century and the first decade or so of the twentieth; a conception based upon the belief in the superior ability of the Teutonic as opposed to the Latin races, in accordance with which the latter were regarded as ' a sort of luxurious and yet impecunious remnant left over from a lazier age, and incapable of effort and efficiency, capable only of gesticulating over organs and ice-cream carts ', and associated in people's minds with ' knives, rags, romantic passions, reckless behaviour, garlic and guitars '.

In no sphere was this Nordic theory so insistently proclaimed, so widely accepted, as in music. Mr. Chesterton's picture may be overdrawn and exaggerated in reference to literature, art, science, politics, philosophy, or any other branch of intellectual activity, but so far as music at least is concerned he even falls short of the actual truth. Music, indeed, during the second part of last century was regarded, in this country at least, as an almost exclusively Teutonic thing. It was grudgingly conceded that Italians had occasionally made useful contributions to the progress of the art in the early stages of its development, but all the greatest achievements of its maturity were claimed to be German. The essentially frivolous and shallow Latins, it was held, were at a permanent disadvantage in competing with the *tief* and *ernst* Teutons. ' They were easily pleased, and so they were easily passed in the race by those who required something of a higher order to satisfy their sense of responsibility (!) . . . The power of strenuous persistence in climbing up the steep ascent of art to higher things was not for them, but for a race whose musical story is the very strongest contrast to theirs, and illustrates the persistent and patient and unweariable devotion to an ideal which was totally different throughout.' Thus Sir Hubert Parry, in his *Style in Musical Art*, one of the standard historical studies of the early twentieth century, and his conception of the noble Teuton, puffing and blowing up the slopes of Mount

Parnassus while the indolent and superficial Latin remained sitting at the foot, strumming on his guitar, was endorsed by almost all writers on music of the period. In accordance with this view Bach and Mozart ' summed up ' everything of value in the work of their respective Italian predecessors, adding something of which the latter were congenitally incapable, while from the time of Beethoven onwards, Italy failed even to provide material worth improving on, and practically ceased to exist as a musical country. With Rossini, Bellini, and Donizetti, indeed, music was commonly held to have reached its nadir, and Verdi was only tolerated on account of his last works, *Aida, Otello, Falstaff*, in which, recognizing the error of his ways, he made a belated endeavour to emulate the nobler and loftier ideals of his German colleagues, and of Wagner in particular. Turning his back on the garlic-scented melodies and the guitar-like orchestration of his earlier operas he set to work manfully in an attempt to produce something not altogether unworthy of a German composer. One is given to understand, of course, that it was not done well, as Dr. Johnson said of a dog walking on its hind legs, but one was surprised to find it being done at all. Nevertheless, it had to be admitted that the spectacle of the aged and venerable sinner creeping penitently on his knees to the shrine of Bayreuth was very touching, and deserved appreciation even to the extent of allowing these later works a humble place by the side of the incomparably greater achievement of the German master. As for the rest of his output, however, it was contemptuously dismissed as consisting of mere successions of vulgar ear-tickling tunes without any musical or dramatic significance whatever.

Such was the conception of musical history, and such the official critical attitude to Verdi, which prevailed, in this country at least, right down to 1914, and they are even still to be met with in academic circles. The reaction, moreover, which started about the beginning of the century against German music, chiefly in France and Russia, did not bring with it a corresponding revulsion in favour of Italy; indeed, the contempt of the Franco-Russian school and its adherents for the Italian operatic composers of the preceding century exceeded, if anything, that of the Germans themselves.

So far as Verdi was concerned it was even more complete, since it embraced the later works also, in which he was supposed—wrongly—to have followed Teutonic ideals to a certain extent. And if, in the years immediately following the war, it became fashionable in certain circles to affect an admiration for Verdi, this was simply part of the perversity of the times. People who found him ' amusing '—the favourite adjective of the period—did so because they honestly believed that his music was thoroughly bad; accepting, in fact, the standard of values already prevailing, and merely inverting it mechanically. The most perfect example of this is afforded by the comic dictum of Stravinsky to the effect that early Verdi is good, but the later Verdi bad.

This, then, was the position until about a year or two ago, when a most remarkable thing happened—the last thing on earth anyone could have expected, namely, the sudden rise of a great wave of enthusiasm for his music, originating in, of all unlikely places, Germany; manifesting itself not only in popular but also in critical and enlightened favour, and not confined merely to his later works—that one could more easily have understood—but embracing the greater part of his output. This revival of interest in Verdi, moreover, is no longer limited to Germany, but appears to be spreading everywhere. In this country, for example, the production of several of his operas, including the little-known *La Forza del Destino*, has been the outstanding success of the Italian season at Covent Garden this year, and two books dealing with the man and his work have made their appearance within a few months of each other; one by Mr. F. Bonavia, and another, the more recent and more important of the two, by Mr. Francis Toye.

This book is more than welcome if only because no satisfactory full-length study of the master has hitherto appeared in English. It is probably even the best book on Verdi that has appeared in any language, though that is not saying very much, for the literature that he has hitherto evoked in Italian, German, and French, is singularly uninteresting and uninspiring. The truth is that Verdi is not an easy or a grateful subject for either biographer or music critic. His life was entirely devoid of the sensational incidents which make the biographies of Wagner, Berlioz, or Liszt such entertaining reading, and his music is so direct, so simple, so unsophisticated, that there is really very little that one can profitably say about it. If Mr. Toye's book, then, is also, like its fellows, apt to be a trifle flat and pedestrian, this is largely on account of the nature of his subject. Even a Strachey, a Maurois, a Ludwig, would find it difficult to make Verdi's life dramatic or picturesque, and certainly no music critic can say much about the music that the ordinary, uninstructed listener cannot perfectly well see for himself. As a repository of facts, however, painstakingly collected and lucidly presented, Mr. Toye's study is invaluable and should be in the hands of all music-lovers. On the critical side one is glad to note that he gives the lie direct to the insinuation, so often repeated as to have become a veritable *cliché*, that the miraculous second flowering of Verdi's genius in his old age was due to the influence of Wagner. Mr. Toye rightly points out that *Aida*, *Otello*, *Falstaff*, are only the logical outcome of what had gone before, and would have been written even if Wagner had never lived.

The chief significance, indeed, of the present Verdi Renaissance is that it signals the definite passing of the oppressive Wagnerian domination which has weighed upon operatic form like an incubus for the last fifty years, and the fact that it should have originated in Germany itself only serves to emphasize this significance. It is also a healthy symptom in other ways, for it indicates a strong reaction on the part of both popular and critical opinion against excessive cerebralism on the one hand and excessive sensationalism on the other; against the tendencies, in fact, which may be conveniently identified with Schönberg and Stravinsky, respectively, and in favour of the predominance of melody over all other elements in the musical synthesis as opposed to the primarily harmonic interest of the former and the rhythmic obsessions of the latter.

Whether this remarkable revival of interest in Verdi will prove to be permanent or not remains to be seen. But even if it should only be temporary it is an exceedingly propitious sign—the first that has appeared upon the musical horizon for many a long day.

1931

Carlo Gesualdo, Prince of Venosa; Musician and Murderer

HIS MOST Illustrious and Serene Highness Don Carlo, third Prince of Venosa, eighth Count of Consa, fifteenth Lord of Gesualdo, Marquis of Laino, Rotondo and S. Stefano, Duke of Caggiano, Lord of Frigento, Acquaputida, Paterno, S. Manco, Boneto, Luceria, S. Lupolo, etc., was descended from one of the oldest and noblest families in the kingdom of the Two Sicilies. The first mention of the name of Gesualdo in Neapolitan history dates back to the Dark Ages which intervene between the fall of Rome and the establishment of the medieval Empire by Charlemagne, and to the time of the ancient kingdom of the Lombards. During the siege of Benevento by Constans II, Emperor of Byzantium, Duke Romualdo, who was in command of the city, finding himself hard pressed, resolved to send his trusty servant Gesualdo to his father Grimoaldo, King of Lombardy, for assistance. Gesualdo accomplished the first part of his task successfully, and a large army was got together by the king in order to march to the assistance of his son. In the meanwhile, Gesualdo was sent back to announce the approach of reinforcements, but had the misfortune to fall into the hands of the besiegers. Thereupon the Greek Emperor suggested to his prisoner that he should go up underneath the walls of the beleaguered city and declare to the Duke his master that he had been unable to obtain reinforcements, and that the only course left open was to surrender the city. For this act of treachery great rewards were promised him. Seeming to comply with the suggestion, Gesualdo was led out by his captors to within hailing distance of the walls, but instead of delivering the false message as he had agreed to do, he spoke to the Duke as follows: ' My lord, take heart, because this night the valiant Grimoaldo, your father, together with the flower of his troops, is encamped upon the banks of the River Sangro, and will speedily fall upon these barbarous invaders who will be forced to take refuge in flight if they are to escape the sharp points of the avenging Lombard spears. Wherefore I beseech you that my wife and children be commended to your care and protection, because this ruffianly crew, finding themselves to be deceived by me in not giving you false information, will without doubt slay me.'

In this Gesualdo guessed aright. His head was cut off and fired by a catapult into the city where it was taken to the Duke, who with great respect kissed it and set upon it his ducal crown. And this, according to some, was the reason for the presence of a ducal crown on the family coat of arms, and the origin of the illustrious house which ever afterwards claimed as their ancestor this Gesualdo 'who for this glorious act of devotion deserves to be numbered among the noblest heroes renowned in story'.

The chronicles go on to say that after this vile and barbarous act, Constans precipitately raised the siege and retired on Naples. A body of Lombards, under the command of Count Capo Mitola, burning with righteous zeal to revenge the death of Gesualdo, and to punish the perfidious Greek, caught up with and attacked the Imperial rearguard and cut it to pieces, none thereof escaping. And this, according to the testimony of Paulus Diaconus, took place near the River Calore.

Although this Gesualdo has generally been considered to be the founder of the noble family which bears his name, he does not seem to be a direct ancestor, at least in the male line, for in subsequent chronicles one reads of a Guglielmo lord of Gesualdo and son of Roger Duke of Puglia, who was the illegitimate son of the great Robert Guiscard, the Norman conqueror of Southern Italy in the eleventh century. This origin of the family is confirmed by inscriptions on buildings and tombstones dedicated to its members. On the other hand, it is quite probable that the title and estate of Gesualdo came to this Guglielmo through his marriage with a female heiress of the earlier Lombard dynasty.

From this time onward the name of Gesualdo occurs frequently in the pages of Neapolitan history. The son of Guglielmo, named Elia, took the side of the Pope in the great struggle of Manfred with the Church, and was consequently deprived of his honours by the king and banished from Naples. On Manfred's downfall he was reinstated. His son Niccolo was a great warrior and captain of the City of Naples and its district; another Elia was Grand Constable and Marshal of the kingdom in 1183; another Niccolo was Captain General and Justiciary of the Basilicata and Regent of the Vicaria in 1290; and Ruggiero was Marshal of the kingdom and Justiciary of Otranto 1385. We also read that Ladislaus, the first king of Naples belonging to the house of Aragon (c. 1400), a great lover of jousting, was thrown to earth by a Gesualdo of Gesualdo, ' a youth of monstrous strength and great skill, who in jousting and martial feats unhorsed every adversary by the strength of his lance and the force of his arm '.

In 1494, Luigi, eleventh Lord of Gesualdo, and third Count of Consa, took part in a rebellion against the king, Ferrante II, and was deprived of his feudal rights. Two years later he was forgiven and reinstated in his privileges, and promptly proceeded to rebel again. Accordingly the king, then Federico of Aragon, gave to his captain Gonsalvo Fernandez de Cordoba the city of Consa, together with the castles of Sant Andria and Santa Mena and other possessions formerly appertaining to the house of Gesualdo. However, this period of disgrace and eclipse did not last long. In 1506, as the result of an agreement arrived at by France and Spain, the house of Gesualdo received back its lands and fortresses, and in 1546 the principality of Venosa was added to its territorial possessions.

The family distinguished itself in other fields besides the field of battle. Ascanio was Archbishop of Bari, and Alfonso was Cardinal Archbishop of Naples, and at one time had a good chance of being made Pope.[1] From a dedication of a book of madrigals by Gasparo della Porta to the aforementioned Ascanio we learn that ' The family of Gesualdo has always held in esteem the art of music, and many knights and princes who have adorned every age, have often exchanged the pen for the sword, and musical instruments for the pen, as witness whereof the most excellent Prince of Venosa '— the subject of the present study. His father, Fabrizio, according

---

[1] A less creditable member of the family figures in a *novella* of Bandello (Part II, No. 7), entitled, *L'Abbate Gesualdo vuol rapir una giovane, e resta vituperosamente da lei ferito, et ella, saltata nel fiume, s'aiuta* (The Abbe Gesualdo, in attempting to molest a young woman, was grievously wounded by her, while she, leaping into the river, effected her escape).

a contemporary writer, Ammirato (*Delle famiglie nobili di Napoli*), was ' greatly appreciative of music, and in this noble art one finds many learned compositions of his which are held in great esteem by the *cognoscenti*. Moreover, he maintained in his own house an academy of all the musicians of the city, whom he supported and favoured most courteously '. But I am inclined to think that the writer has, to a certain extent at least, confused the father with the son, for nowhere else does one find it mentioned that Fabrizio was a composer. Nevertheless, it is certain that he was a prince of great culture and refinement. He had four children—two sons, Luigi and Carlo, and two daughters, Isabella and Vittoria.

Carlo, born about 1560 (some say 1557), was the second son, and consequently was not heir to the title and family estates. He seems to have evinced early in life a remarkable aptitude for music which could only have been intensified and stimulated by his environment and opportunities. He is said to have been taught by Pomponio Nenna, but considering that the latter was only born in 1560, or possibly even later, this seems improbable. However that may be, he learnt composition and received instruction in the playing of several instruments. As an executant and improviser he rapidly attained to great proficiency; he was particularly renowned as a performer on the *arciliuto*, or bass-lute. In fact, his early reputation seems to be rather that of an executant than a composer, and of a musical Maecenas and art patron. A contemporary writer on music, Scipione Cerreto, in his book entitled *Della prattica Musica, vocale et Strumentale*, says of him: ' Not only did this Prince take great delight in music, but also for his pleasure and entertainment did keep at his court, at his own expense, many excellent composers, players and singers; so that I do often think that if this nobleman had lived at the time of the Greeks of antiquity, when one who was ignorant of music was considered uneducated, however great his knowledge of other things (as witness whereof the story of the philosopher Themistocles who was greatly discomfited and put to shame for not being able, at a certain banquet, to play upon some instrument) they would have raised up unto his memory a statue, not of mere marble, but of purest gold.'

The names of many members of this private academy, or

camerata—strikingly similar to the more famous one of Count Bardi in Florence at the same time—are known to us. Chief among them are Scipione Stella, a composer; Giandomenico Montella, organist, harpist, and lutenist; Fabrizio Filomarino, a skilled performer on the seven-stringed guitar; Scipione Dentice, a writer on music and player of the *cembalo*, who published five books of madrigals between 1591 and 1607; Antonio Grifone, a violist; Rocco Rodio, one of the most distinguished musicians of his time, especially on the theoretical side; and Leonardo Primavera dell' Arpa, also one of the most eminent composers and executants of the period.

This *camerata* was not exclusively musical, however. Many poets used to be present at its gatherings, among them Torquato Tasso, the foremost poet of his age. He seems to have been at that time staying with Count Manso, the same whom Milton visited during his Italian travels, and to whom he addressed the Latin poem beginning

> Haec quoque, Manse, tuae meditantur carmina laudi

and the Count seems also to have been a friend of Gesualdo.[1] The latter met Tasso about Easter in 1588, and a close friendship was established between them which was only terminated by the poet's death in 1595. Three of the latter's poems are addressed to Gesualdo—the sonnets, which begin with the lines ' *Alta prole di regi eletta in terra* ' and ' *Carlo, il vostro leon c'ha nero il vello* ' (an allusion to the heraldic device of the Gesualdo family, a black lion with five red lilies upon a silver field), and a *canzone* in which are celebrated his most distinguished ancestors. There is little doubt, moreover, that this friendship played a very important part in Gesualdo's artistic career. In the first place, Tasso was the greatest living exponent of the literary form known as the madrigal. From 1592 onwards he sent his noble friend no less than forty examples, written expressly for him to set to music, eight of which are actually among the Prince's published compositions: namely, *Gelo ha*

[1] It is interesting to note that in 1638 Milton sent home from Venice a number of books, ' particularly a chest or two of choice music-books of the best masters flourishing about that time in Italy—namely Luca Marenzio, Monte Verdi, Horatio Vecchi, Cifra, *the Prince of Venosa* and several others ' (*vide* W. Godwin, *Lives of Edward and John Philips*, Appendix II).

Madonna il seno, Mentre Madonna, Se da si nobil mano, Felice primavera, Caro amoroso meo, Se cosi dolce e il duolo, Se taccio il duol s'avanza, Non e questo la mano. It is quite possible that others of the forty were also set to music by Gesualdo, but have not survived. It is certainly beyond doubt that the prevailing spirit of his music, its passionate sorrow, elegiac tenderness, and eloquent despair, are essentially a musical paraphrase or reproduction of the spirit of Tasso's poetry.

The young prince, together with his illustrious friend and members of the *camerata*, would often retire to his castle of S. Antonio in Mergellina, just outside Naples; and they would spend whole nights out in the bay, singing *villotte*, and madrigals, the prince accompanying himself on the lute.

Somewhere about the year 1585 an event took place which was destined to be the cause of a terrible tragedy in Carlo's life. This event was the death of his elder brother Luigi, in virtue of which Carlo became the heir to the title and estates of the house of Gesualdo. It was therefore incumbent upon him to marry and produce descendants unless the direct line was to be extinguished and the estates dispersed. One can be fairly certain that the idea of marriage was uncongenial to his temperament, for at a time when the nobility were accustomed to marry at an extremely early age, Carlo had remained single until close on thirty. We are told too, by a contemporary writer, that he cared for nothing but music (*non si diletta d'altro che di musica*). However, the obligations of his position proved stronger than his personal inclinations, and in 1586 he was married to his first cousin, Donna Maria d'Avalos, who, though only twenty-one, had already been married twice, and, what was essential, ' *havea dati segni sufficienti di fecondità* ',[1] as the chronicler Ammirato observes.

All contemporary chroniclers are agreed on one point, namely, the ' surprising beauty ' of Donna Maria, one of them even going so far as to say that she was reputed to be the most beautiful woman in the kingdom of the Two Sicilies. This may seem to us somewhat excessive praise if the portrait of her which has survived in the church of San Domenico Maggiore at Naples is at all like

[1] ' had already given sufficient proofs of fruitfulness '.

her. There she seems rather plain and ordinary, as many famous beauties of bygone ages do in their portraits. Her first husband, whom she married at the early age of fifteen, was Federico Carafa, son of Ferrante Carafa, Marquis of S. Lucido, 'admired by the whole nobility as an angel from Heaven', writes the rapturous and fulsome Ammirato. They had two children, but after three years Federico died suddenly, '*forse per aver troppo reiterare con quella i congiungimenti carnali*', says another indiscreet chronicler. Two years later the young widow married Don Alfonso, son of the Marquis di Giuliano, who seems to have had a stronger constitution, or possibly greater moderation and prudence, for in 1586 a papal dispensation for divorce was granted, followed almost immediately by her marriage to Carlo Gesualdo.

The wedding was celebrated with truly regal magnificence, we are told, and feasting and rejoicing in the palace of San Severo, where the prince lived, continued for many days.

The marriage appears to have been extremely happy for some three or four years—which seems about as long as Donna Maria could endure one husband—and a son, Don Emmanuele, was born to them. (As we shall see later there was possibly also a second child.) And then, in the year 1590, occurred the terrible event in Gesualdo's life to which allusion has been made.

The main sources of our information concerning the tragedy are two; firstly, a chronicle of the time called the MS. Corona; secondly, the *Informatione presa dalla Gran Corte della Vicaria*. With the aid of these two valuable documents we are able to reconstruct the whole drama with considerable accuracy, although, as will be seen, they differ slightly on certain points. The first deals more fully with the events which led up to the tragedy, the second with the tragedy itself. Apart from their biographical relevance to our subject, they also afford us a fascinating insight into the life and manners of the times, and for that reason alone would deserve attention. The translations which follow are by no means literal. I have preferred to sacrifice verbal accuracy to the preservation, where possible, of the colour and atmosphere of the originals.

'The enemy of the human race, unable to endure the spectacle of such great love and happiness, such conformity of tastes and

163

desires in two married people, awakened in the bosom of Donna Maria impure desires and a libidinous and unbridled appetite for the sweetnesses of illicit love and for the beauty of a certain knight. This was Fabrizio Carafa, third Duke of Andria and seventh Count of Ruovo, reputed to be the handsomest and most accomplished nobleman of the city, in age not yet arrived at the sixth lustre, in manners so courteous and gracious, and of appearance so exquisite that from his features one would say that he was an Adonis; from his manner and bearing, a Mars. He had already long been married to Donna Maria Carafa, daughter of Don Luigi, Prince of Stigliano, a lady not only of great beauty but also of supreme goodness, by whom he had four children.'

The equality of age in the two lovers, the similarity of their tastes, the numerous occasions presented by balls and feasts, the equal desire of both parties to take pleasure in each other, were all tinder to the fire which burnt in their breasts. The first messengers of their mutual flames were their eyes, which betrayed to their hearts with flashes of lightning the Etna which each cherished for the other. From glances they passed to words, from words to letters, given to and received by faithful messengers, in which they invited each other to sweet combat in the lists of love. The Archer, though reputed blind, was a very Argus in finding opportunities for coupling the two lovers, and knew well how to find a convenient place of meeting for the first occasion of their coming together, which was in a garden in the Borgo di Chiaia, in the pavilion whereof the Duke did lie concealed, awaiting his beloved who, on pretext of diversion and entertainment, was taken there. And she, while walking there, affected to be overcome by some bodily pain, and separating herself from her escort, entered into the pavilion wherein lay the Duke, who, without the loss of one moment, put into execution the work of love. Nor was this the only occasion on which they came together for these enjoyments, but many and many times did they do so for many months in various and diverse places according to the opportunities provided by fortune. Most frequently it was in the palace of the Princess, even in her very bedchamber, through the aid of her maid-servant, that they did dally amorously together. This practice, having become frequent and familiar, came to the ears of relations and friends of the Prince, amongst others to those of Don Giulio Gesualdo, uncle of the Prince Don Carlo. This Don Giulio had himself been fiercely enamoured of the charms of Donna Maria, and had left no stone unturned in order to attain his desire; but, having been several times reproached by her for his foolish frenzy and warned that if he persisted in such thoughts and intentions she would divulge all to the Prince her husband, the unhappy Don Giulio, seeing that neither by gifts nor by entreaties nor by tears could he hope to win her to his desires, did cease to importune her, believing her to be a chaste Penelope. But when whispers came to his ears concerning the loves and pleasures of Donna Maria and the Duke, and after that he had assured himself of their truth with his own eyes from more than one certain sign, such was the wrath and fury which assailed him on finding that the strumpet did lie with others, that, without losing one moment of time, he straightway revealed all to the Prince. On hearing such grievous tidings, Don Carlo did at first seem more dead than alive; but, lest he should seem to place credence too lightly in the asseverations of others, he resolved to assure himself of the truth of the matter himself.

In the meanwhile the lovers had been warned that their secret was known, whereupon the Duke gave pause to his pleasures; but Donna Maria, unable to endure this remission, solicited the Duke that they should resume them again. He then made known to her that their guilty passion had been detected, and represented to her the dangers to both honour and life which would ensue to both alike if they did not keep their crapulous desires under control.

In reply to these prudent reasonings, the Princess answered that if his heart was capable of fear he had better become a lackey; that nature had erred in creating a knight with the spirit of a woman, and in creating in her a woman with the spirit of a valorous knight. It did not behove him to reveal the vileness and cowardice of a common man, and if he were capable of sheltering fear in his heart he had better banish from it his love for her and never come into her presence again.

At this angry reply, which touched him to the very quick, the Duke went in person to the offended lady, and spoke to her as follows: 'Fair lady, if you would that I should die for love of you, I shall be greatly honoured in being the victim of your beauty. I have the courage to meet my death, but not the constancy to endure yours. For if I die, assuredly you will not live. This is my fear which makes me coward; I have not strength to endure this blow. If you see no way to avert a calamity, give me at least the assurance that the Duke of Andria alone will be the victim of your husband's vengeance, and then I shall let you see whether I am afraid of steel. You are too cruel, not to me, who still finds you too merciful, but to your own beauty, in exposing it thus to moulder away before its due time in the darkness and silence of the tomb.'

To these words the Princess made answer thus: 'My lord Duke, one moment of your absence is more death-dealing to me than a thousand deaths which might come to me through my delights. If I die with you I shall nevermore be separated from you, but if you go away from me I shall die far apart from all that my heart holds dear, which is your self. Make up your mind, then, either to show yourself faithless by departing from me, or to prove yourself loyal by not abandoning me. As for the reasons which you have given me, you should have taken thought of them before, not when the arrow has sped and it is too late. I have courage enough and strength enough to endure the cold steel, but not the bitter frost of your absence. You had no right to love me, nor I to love you, if we were capable of entertaining such base and cowardly thoughts. To conclude—I so wish and so command, and to my order I brook no reply unless that you would lose me for ever.'

To this impassioned speech the unhappy Duke, bowing humbly in token of submission, replied: 'Since you wish to die, I shall die with you; such is your wish, so be it.'

And so did they continue in their delights.

The Prince, now alert and on the watch, having had all the locks of the doors in the palace secretly removed or damaged, and particularly those of the rooms wherein the Princess was wont to dally amorously with her paramour, gave out one day his intention of going to the chase, as was his custom, declaring also that he would not return that evening. Accordingly he set out in hunting attire and on horseback, accompanied by a numerous retinue of intimates and followers, and made as if to go to that place known as Gli Astroni, having previously left orders with some of his servants who were privy to the secret, to leave open at night all the necessary doors, but in such wise that they should yet retain the appearance of being closed. Then the Prince took his departure, and went to conceal himself in the house of one of his relations.

The Duke, having learnt that the Prince had departed upon a hunting expedition and would not return that evening, set forth at four hours of the night[1] in search of his usual pleasures, and was received by Donna Maria with her wonted affection. And after that they had solaced themselves at their ease, they fell asleep and thereby lost both body and soul. For in the meanwhile the Prince, having returned secretly to the palace at midnight, accompanied by a troup of armed men chosen from among his intimates, made his way rapidly to the bedchamber of the Princess, and with one blow broke open the door. Entering furiously he discovered the lovers in bed together; at which sight the state of mind of the unhappy prince can be imagined. But quickly shaking off the dejection into which this miserable spectacle had plunged him, he slew with innumerable dagger thrusts the sleepers before they had time to waken.

And after he had ordered that their dead bodies should be dragged from the room and left exposed, he made a statement of his reasons for this butchery, and departed with his familiars to his city of Venosa.

And this tragedy took place on the night of the 16 October 1590. The bodies of the wretched lovers remained exposed all the following morning in the midst of the hall, and all the city flocked to see the pitiful sight.

The lady's wounds were all in the belly, and more particularly in those parts which she ought to have kept honest; and the Duke was wounded even more grievously.

Too beautiful, too alike, too unfortunate were this unhappy pair.

[1] The first hour of the night is 6.30—7.30 by our time. Consequently four hours of the night is 9.30.

At the hour of vespers the bodies were removed for burial amidst the lamentations of the entire city.

Such was the end of impure desires.'

That is all we learn from the *Successi tragici et amorosi de Silvio ed Ascanio Corona.* The Venetian ambassador to Naples mentions a few other details in one of his communications to his government. After giving a succinct account of the tragedy, he adds that ' these three princely families (i.e. Gesualdo, d'Avalos, and Carafa) were intimately connected with and related to almost all the other noble families of the kingdom, and everyone seems stunned by the horror of this event. The illustrious Lord Viceroy himself was greatly dismayed at the news, for he loved and greatly esteemed the Duke as a man who both by nature and through application was the possessor of all the most noble and worthy qualities which appertain to a prince and a valorous gentleman. Various ministers of justice, together with officials of the Courts have been to the palace, and after making various inquiries commanded that all persons connected with the case should be sequestered and guarded in their own houses; but up to the present, nothing more has been heard of the matter.'

And now we come to the verbatim report of the proceedings of the Grand Court of the Vicaria, a copy of which, by a rare stroke of good fortune, is still extant, although the original document has disappeared from the Neapolitan Archives.

It consists of three separate depositions: first, that of the examining magistrates and officials; secondly, the narrative of the servant-in-waiting to Donna Maria; and thirdly, and most interesting, the evidence of Don Carlo's personal servant. Many details in these will be found at variance with the account given already; where these discrepancies occur, it is only natural that we should give the preference to the official narrative. For example, the trap laid by the Prince by announcing his intention of going hunting—so reminiscent of the device of the Sultan Schahriar in the *Arabian Nights*—is clearly erroneous.

' *Informatione presa dalla Gran Corte della Vicaria. Die* 27 *octobris,* 1590, *in quo habitat Don Carolus Gesualdus.*'[1]

---

[1] Evidence taken by the Grand Court of the Vicaria the 27 October 1590 in the house of Don Carlo Gesualdo.

' As it has been brought to the notice of the Grand Court of the Vicaria that in the house of the most illustrious Don Carlo Gesualdo, in the place of S. Domenico Maggiore, the illustrious Lady Donna Maria d'Avalos, wife of the said Don Carlo, and the illustrious Don Fabrizio Carafa, Duke of Andria, had been done to death: the illustrious gentlemen Don Giovan Tommaso Salamanca, Fulvio di Costanzo, Royal Councillors and Criminal Judges of the Grand Court, the Magnificent Fiscal Procurator, and I, the undersigned Master of the Grand Court, held conference in the house of the aforesaid Don Carlo Gesualdo. On entering into the upper apartments of the said house, in the furthest room thereof, was found dead, stretched out upon the ground, the most illustrious Don Fabrizio Carafa, Duke of Andria. The only clothing upon the body was a woman's nightdress, worked with lace, with a collar of black silk and with one sleeve red with blood, and the said Duke of Andria was covered with blood and wounded in many places, as follows: an arquebus wound in the left arm passing from one side of the elbow to the other and also through the breast, the sleeve of the said nightdress being scorched; many and divers wounds in the chest made by sharp steel weapons, also in the arms, in the head, and in the face; and another arquebus wound in the temple above the left eye whence there was an abundant flow of blood. And in the self-same room was found a gilt couch with curtains of green cloth, and within the said bed was found dead the above-mentioned Donna Maria d'Avalos clothed in a nightdress, and the bed was filled with blood. On being seen by the aforesaid gentlemen and by me, the aforesaid Master, the body was recognized to be that of Donna Maria d'Avalos, lying dead with her throat cut; also with a wound in the head, in the right temple, a dagger thrust in the face, more dagger wounds in the right hand and arm, and in the breast and flank two sword thrusts. And on the said bed was found a man's shirt with frilled starched cuffs, and on a chair covered in crimson velvet, near the said bed, was discovered a gauntlet of iron, and an iron glove, burnished; also a pair of breeches of green cloth, a doublet of yellow cloth, a pair of green silk hose, a pair of white cloth pantaloons, and a pair of cloth shoes, all of which vestments were without injury, whether sword thrusts or bloodstains. And at

M

the side of the apartment of the lady, the door of the said room was found to be smashed at the foot and could not be closed by means of the handle, for that the injury was made in such a way that it could not lock, nor would the handle hold when placed in the aperture, and likewise the lock of the door had been bent and twisted in such a way that the key could not enter the keyhole, and consequently the said door could not be locked.

' And on entering into the antechamber wherein was the small door opening on to the spiral staircase which led down to the apartment of Don Carlo, Pietro Bardotti, servant-in-waiting to the said Don Carlo Gesualdo, gave up to the said gentlemen a key, saying that when he entered the room where he had found the Lord Duke and Donna Maria d'Avalos lying dead, he found the said key upon a chair beside the bed; and this key, which opened the door of the room of the apartment in the said house, he did declare to be false. And the key being taken by me, hereunder signed Domenico Micene, by order of the above-mentioned gentlemen, the lock of the door in the said room was inspected, and another ordinary key was found in the lock thereof. And on essaying the said key which had been given by the said Pietro, it was found to open the lock of the door in the said room as well as the ordinary key.

' And at the same time by order of the said gentlemen, two coffins were brought into the said room, and with them came the Reverend Father Carlo Mastrillo, a Jesuit father, together with two other Jesuit priests. And when they had washed the body of the said Duke of Andria the following wounds were clearly discerned upon him, namely: arquebus wounds in the left arm, through the elbow and in the flank with two shots, one arquebus wound about the eye from side to side, some of the brains having come out; and he was also wounded in many places in the head, face, neck, chest, stomach, flanks, arms, hands and shoulders—all by sword thrusts, deep, many of them passing through the body from front to back. This body had been found immediately upon entering the said room, three paces distance from the couch wherein lay the said Donna Maria d'Avalos. And underneath the said body were many marks upon the floor made by swords passing through the said body and penetrating deeply into the said floor. And after that the said body had been washed and dressed in a pair of black silk breeches and a jerkin of black velvet, it was taken by the Reverend Don Carlo Mastrillo, who had come to receive the body on behalf of the wife of the said Lord Duke, the Countess of Ruvo his grandmother, and the Lord Prior of Ungheria his uncle. And when it had been placed in a coffin by order of the said illustrious gentlemen, the body was given to the Jesuit fathers above-mentioned, who placed it in a coach and departed with it; and the said clothes which were found upon the chair within the said room, belonging to the said Duke, together with the gauntlet, glove and false key, were consigned unto me, the said Domenico Micene, that I should have them in safe keeping.

' And then there came the illustrious Marchioness di Vico, the aged aunt of the said Donna Maria d'Avalos, in order that she might dress her; and after that she had been dressed by the servants of the house she was placed in the other coffin and consigned to the care of the illustrious Lady Duchess of Traietto, according to the wish and request of the illustrious Lady Sveva Gesualdo, mother of the said Lady Maria, and was carried to the church of S. Domenico.

' And further it is attested that the said Lords Justiciary and the Fiscal Lord Advocate, on descending to the apartment on the middle floor wherein the said Don Carlo is alleged to have slept, found in one of the rooms three halberds, one of which had a twisted point, and all three soiled and stained with blood, and also in the same room a round shield of iron, large, and with black silk fringes, a short sword with a silver hilt, a long sword similarly gilt, and two wax torches which had been left behind in the said house.

' In witness whereof

' *By order of the above-mentioned illustrious gentlemen, I Dominico Micene, Master of the Grand Court, have written the above account with mine own hand.*

' *Evidence examined and taken by me, Master Giovanni Sanchez, with the assistance of Master Mutio Surgenti, fiscal advocate, by order of the Excellent Masters, concerning the death of the illustrious gentleman Don Fabrizio Carafa, Duke of Andria, and of the Lady Maria d'Avalos. The 28 October 1590, in the house of the illustrious*

Duke of Torremaggiore, lately inhabited by Don Carlo Gesualdo and Donna Maria d'Avalos.'

Silvia Albana, aged twenty, being, as she said, maidservant to the aforesaid Lady Maria d' Avalos, and keeper of her wardrobe and of all things which concerned her person, and having served her mistress for six years, bore witness on oath. On being examined and questioned, what did witness know concerning the death of the said Maria d'Avalos, and who killed her, and in what manner? she answered, that the truth of what she knew was as follows:

On the Tuesday evening, which was the twenty-sixth day[1] of the present month, that is, eight days ago, the Lady Donna Maria, after that she had dined, retired to rest at about four hours of the night. Witness, together with one Laura Scala, likewise servant in attendance on the said Lady, did undress her and left her in bed. Whereupon Laura then retired to bed, as she was wont to do, in the room adjoining that wherein the said lady was reposing, and witness set about preparing her garments for the next day.

Then did the said Lady Donna Maria call witness to her; and when she had come into the room, the said lady asked for clothes wherewith to dress herself. And in reply to witness's inquiry why she wished to dress, she made reply that she had heard the whistle of the Duke of Andria and wished to go to the window—which witness had seen the lady do many times before, and on several occasions, when the moon was shining, she, the witness, had seen the Duke of Andria in the street. And she did recognize him by moonlight from having often seen him by daytime, and knew him well, having often heard him conversing with the said lady.

And the said lady having ordered that garments be brought to her, witness brought forth a petticoat and a shawl for her head; and the said lady, being dressed, did go to open the window, and went out upon the balcony, first ordering the said witness to stand on guard and to warn her if she should hear any astir in the house or in the courtyard. And witness did as she was told; and as Lady Maria opened the window she heard five hours of the night striking. After half an hour, that is, at five-and-a-half hours of the

[1] Obviously an error of the copyist.

nigth, the said Lady Donna Maria summoned witness to close the window and to undress her again. Accordingly witness disrobed her; and when that the Lady Donna Maria had retired to bed, she ordered that another nightdress be brought to her, as that which she was wearing was wet with sweat. And witness brought her one which had a collar of worked black silk and a pair of cuffs of the same colour, and left it upon the bed as she was commanded to do—which nightdress witness saw on the Duke of Andria when she discovered him in the morning, in the very room wherein the said Lady Donna Maria did sleep, dead upon the ground, covered with blood, and wounded in many places. And after the said Lady Donna Maria had told her to leave the nightdress which she had brought upon the bed, she asked that a candle might be lit and placed upon the chair; and accordingly witness lit a wax candle and placed it upon the chair. And when witness was retiring for the night the said Lady Donna Maria said to her, 'Shut the door without turning the handle and do not come in, unless I call you'. And witness did as she was told, and as the said Lady Donna Maria had told her not to come in unless she was called, she did not wish to undress but laid herself down upon her bed fully attired, and while reading a book fell asleep.

While still asleep she heard the door of the room wherein she was, which stood at the head of a flight of stairs leading to the middle floor on which the Lord Don Carlo Gesualdo did live, violently opened. And on awakening with a great start it did seem to her as if she were dreaming and did see, while the lamp in the room wherein she lay was going out, three men entering whom witness knew not by sight. And scarcely had she seen them than they approached the room wherein slept the said Lady Donna Maria; and she saw that one of them, who was the last in order, was carrying a halberd, but could not say if the others were carrying arms. And speedily the said men entered into the inner room, and witness heard two loud reports, and almost at the same moment the words, 'There, it is done'. Hardly had she heard these words spoken than by the staircase she perceived the Lord Don Carlo Gesualdo, husband of the Lady Donna Maria, entering the room wherein witness was sleeping; and together with the said Lord Don

173

Carlo came Pietro Bardotti with two lighted torches in his hands. And the said Lord Don Carlo was carrying a halberd, and said to witness, 'Traitress, I shall kill you. This time you shall not escape me.' And having ordered the said Pietro Bardotti not to permit her to depart, he entered into the room of the said Lady Donna Maria. And as he went in, he ordered the said Pietro Bardotti to fix one of the torches which he was carrying at the side of the door. The said Pietro did so, whereat witness fled into the room where the child was, and, lingering there a moment, did hear the said Don Carlo in the room saying, 'Where are they?' And the nurse besought him that for the love of God he would not do hurt to the child. Whereupon the Lord Don Carlo having commanded that the closet in which the lady was wont to keep her jewels should be closed, went out. Then witness, hearing no sounds proceeding from the room, came out from under the bed where she had been hiding and saw the above-mentioned Pietro Bardotti with a lighted torch. And he said to her, ' Do not fear, Don Carlo has departed '. And on witness asking him what had happened, Bardotti replied, ' Both of them are dead '.

Witness had not the courage to enter the room until the morning, when the other servants came up and it was already light; and then they did all go in together and saw the Lady Donna Maria d'Avalos lying dead with many wounds, in her own bed, upon which lay a man's shirt, and on a chair near the bed a pair of green silk knee-breeches, a pair of stockings, and white underclothing; and near the door a dead body with many wounds and covered with blood; and on coming close she recognized it to be the body of the Duke of Andria.

And such was the evidence of witness, who added that the Duke was wearing the lady's nightdress.

On being asked if she could say whether the clothes which were upon the chair were soiled, and to whom they belonged, witness answered that the clothes which she saw were unsoiled and unspotted, and that she believed them to belong to the Duke of Andria, but could not say for certain.

On being asked what time it would have been when the three men of whom she spoke, and Don Carlo after them, came up the staircase, witness replied that when she came out from under the bed, as told above, the clock struck seven.

On being asked whether she knew the whereabouts of Don Carlo Gesualdo, and who had gone with him, witness replied that she did not know, because from the time when they left until Don Giovanni came thither with the other Lords Justiciary and the Fiscal Lord Advocate, she had been kept shut up in the women's apartments, and had not spoken with anyone.

On being asked what had happened to the body of Donna Maria, she said that on the Wednesday morning the Marchioness di Vico had come and had had the body dressed, and witness had helped in so doing; and thus dressed, the body had been placed in a coffin, and she understood that it had been taken to the church of S. Domenico. And this was all she knew. And being asked how the Duke gained entrance, she answered that she did not know.

Silvia Albana bore witness as above.

On the same day and in the same place, Pietro Malitiale, otherwise Bardotti, aged about forty, said that he was in the service of the Lord Don Carlo Gesualdo as a personal servant, and that he had served the family for twenty-eight years. Giving evidence on oath, he was questioned concerning the occurrence and his knowledge thereof, firstly, where at present was Don Carlo, and how long was it since he had seen him? He answered that at the moment he did not know where he was, and that he had not seen him since the Tuesday evening, a week past; and that on the Wednesday morning, when he left, it would be about seven hours of the night. He had departed on horseback, but witness himself did not see his departure.

On being asked why Don Carlo left that night, and with whom he had gone, he replied: ' My Lords, I shall tell you the truth. On the Tuesday evening, which was the twenty-sixth day of the present month, the said Lord Don Carlo dined at three hours of the night in his apartments on the middle floor, undressed himself, and retired to bed as he was wont to do every evening; and those who served him at supper were witness, Pietro de Vicario, a man-servant, Alessandro Abruzzese, and a young priest who was a musician. And when he had finished dinner the aforesaid Pietro de Vicario and the others departed while witness remained behind to lock the door. After he had secured the door the Lord Don Carlo composed himself to slumber, and witness covered him up and, after undressing, went to bed. Being thus asleep, it would be about six hours of the night when he heard the Lord Don Carlo calling for him that he should bring him a glass of water. Witness went to the well to draw water, and when he had descended to the courtyard he noticed that the postern gate, opening on to the street, was open at that late hour. And on taking up the water he beheld Don Carlo up and dressed in doublet and hose. And he told witness to give him also his long cloak to put on. When witness asked him whither he was going at such a late hour of the night, he replied that he was going a-hunting; and on witness observing that it was not the time for going to the chase, the said Lord Don Carlo replied to him: " You shall see what hunting I am going to do." So saying he finished dressing, and told witness to light two torches; which done, the said Lord Don Carlo drew from beneath the bed a curved sword which he gave to witness to carry under his arm, also a dagger and a poignard together with an arquebus. Taking with him all these weapons, he went to the staircase which led up to the apartment of the Lady Donna Maria d'Avalos, and while mounting by it the said Lord Don Carlo spoke to the witness, saying: " I am going to massacre the Duke of Andria and that strumpet Donna Maria." And while mounting the stairs, witness saw three men, each of whom was carrying a halberd and an arquebus; which men, witness attested, threw open the door at the head of the stairs which led to the apartments of Donna Maria. And when the three men had entered into the said apartment of Donna Maria, the Lord Don Carlo said to them: " Slay that scoundrel together with that strumpet! Shall a Gesualdo be made cuckold? " (*A casa Gesualdo corna.*) Then witness heard the sound of firearms, but heard no voices, because he had remained outside the room. After that he had remained a short while thus, the three men came out, and he recognized one of them to be Pietro de Vicario, manservant, another to be Ascanio Lama, and the third to be a confidential servant called Francesco; and they de-

parted by the same staircase by which they had come up armed.
Then Don Carlo himself came out, his hands covered with blood;
but he turned back and re-entered the chamber of Donna Maria,
saying: " I do not believe they are dead." Then the said witness
entered with a torch and perceived a dead body near the door. The
said Don Carlo went up to the bed of the Lady Donna Maria and
dealt her still more wounds, saying: " I do not believe she is dead."
He then commanded witness not to let the women scream, and the
said Lord Don Carlo Gesualdo descended the staircase by which
he had come; and witness heard a great noise of horses below, and
in the morning saw neither the Lord Don Carlo, nor his confidential servant, nor any of the members of the Court or of the
household of the Lord Don Carlo.

' And this is that which the witness knew.

' *Signum crucis.*'

So ends the *Informatione presa dalla Gran Corte della Vicaria.*
The copyist of the document adds that the inquiry was discontinued
at the command of the Viceroy, in view of the manifest justification
for the Prince's act in slaying the Duke of Andria and his own
erring spouse. But this would seem merely to be a personal opinion
of the scribe, and not at all in accordance with the general sentiment which, as we shall see, was ranged almost unanimously on
the side of the guilty pair.

Other accounts of this terrible deed are to be found, with slightly
varying details, in the minor literature of the time, but none of them
are so authentic or circumstantial as the two above reproduced.
Mention, however, should be made of the version of Brantôme in
his celebrated *chronique scandaleuse,* the *Vies des Dames Galantes*
(*Discours premier, sur les dames qui font l'amour et leurs maris cocus*).
After describing the occurrence with many inaccuracies, he adds
that:

' Il y eut des parens de ladite dame morte qui en furent très-
dolents et très-estomacqués, jusques à s'en vouloir ressentir par la
mort et le meurtre, ainsi que la loy du pays le porte, mais d'autant
qu'elle avoit esté tuée par des marauts de valets et esclaves qui ne
méritoient d'avoir leurs mains teintes d'un si beau et si noble sang,
et sur ce seul sujet s'en vouloient ressentir et rechercher le

mary, fust par justice ou autrement, et non s'il eust fait le coup luy-mesme de sa propre main; car n'en fust esté autre chose, ny recherché.

' Voilà une sotte et bizarre opinion et formalisation, dont je m'en rapporte à nos grand discoureurs et bons jurisconsultes, pour sçavoir, quel acte est plus énorme, de tuer sa femme de sa propre main qui l'a tante aimé, ou de celle d'un maraut esclave.

' Il y a force raisons à déduire là-dessus, dont je me passeray de les alléguer, craignant qu'elles soyent trop foibles au prix de celles de ces grands.

' J'ay ouy conter que le viceroy, en sçachant la conjuration, en advertit l'amant, voire l'amante; mais telle estoit leur destinée, qui se devoit ainsi finer par si belles amours.

' Cette dame estoit fille de dom Carlo d'Avalos, second frère du marquis de Pescayre, auquel, si on eust fait un pareil tour en aucunes de ses amours que je sçay, il y a long-temps qu'il fust esté mort.'[1]

Another and greater French writer, Anatole France, made the tragic occurrence the subject of one of his finest short stories, entitled: ' Histoire de Doña Maria d'Avalos et de Don Fabricio Duc d'Andria.' It is to be found in the volume entitled *Le Puits de Sainte Claire*, but as it is almost entirely a work of imagination it does not concern us here.

The San Severo palace in the Piazza San Domenico where the

[1] There were some among the relatives of the said lady who were deeply grieved and offended thereat, even to the point of wishing to revenge themselves by death and murder, according to the laws of the country; all the more because she had been done to death by knaves and servants whose hands were unworthy to shed such fair and noble blood, and for this reason alone they would have had vengeance upon the husband, either by law or otherwise, and not if he had dealt the stroke with his own hand; but nought came of it.

Here indeed is a crazy and extravagant notion, concerning which I invite the judgement of our great lawyers and good juris consults: namely, whether it is more monstrous to kill the wife you have loved by your own hand or by that of a vile lackey.

Many arguments can be brought forward on this score which I will forbear to mention, fearing that they should seem trivial beside those of such eminent persons.

I have heard it said that the Viceroy warned her and her lover on hearing of the plot which was afoot; but such was their destiny, and the fated end of such sweet loves.

This lady was daughter to Don Carlo d'Avalos, second brother of the Marquis of Pescara, who would himself have long been dead if any such misfortune had befallen him in any of his amours of which I have heard tell.

tragic event took place, still exists, although the great earthquake of 1688 which devastated Naples necessitated its restoration.

It is related that after the flight of the Prince, the palace was closed and remained unoccupied for a considerable time; but that every night at the hour of midnight the people who lived in the vicinity would hear a loud and anguished cry, and the white phantom of Donna Maria would be seen gliding in the darkness through the alleys and passages which surrounded the palace. To this very day the story is told among the common people of Naples, and the palace has never lost its sinister reputation. In recent times the sudden collapse of part of the building, involving loss of life, was at once attributed to the working of a fatal curse which has rested on it throughout the three centuries and more that have passed since the events which we have been narrating took place.

There was another and later inhabitant of the palace, however, to whom part at least of this evil reputation must be ascribed. This was Signor Raimondo di Sangro, Prince of San Severo, who lived there about the middle of the eighteenth century. He seems to have dabbled in science, or alchemy; and during his occupation of the palace wandering tongues of flame and infernal lights were often seen to flicker through the windows on the ground floor, which look out on the Vico San Severo—and sometimes the flames were red, sometimes blue, or even a lurid green, and strange sounds also were to be heard. In the vivid and superstitious imagination of the Neapolitan *lazzarone*, this Prince is represented as a kind of Nostradamus or magician who possessed the power of raising the dead and of fasting indefinitely. He is also said to have been accustomed to drive about over the sea in a carriage drawn by supernatural horses.

But to return to Gesualdo. He went straight to the Viceroy, Don Giovanni Zuniga, Count of Miranda, and acquainted him with what had happened. The Viceroy advised him to put himself out of reach of the relations of the murdered couple, who belonged to two of the richest and most powerful families of the kingdom. The Prince therefore retired to his castle at Gesualdo, which he proceeded to fortify against a possible attack. Indeed, such was his fear of vengeance that he even went so far as to cut down all the forests and thickets which stood around his stronghold, lest they should serve to conceal the approach of hostile forces.

These precautions were not by any means superfluous. The nobility of that time, we are told by a contemporary writer, ' were arrogant and presumptuous, greatly disposed to vengeance ', and particular examples of the length to which affronted honour or *amour propre* would go are so numerous as to be almost common place.

' The exaggerated insistence on the point of honour resulted in many deeds of violence, in brutal and callous murders on the slightest pretext. . . . The Marchese di Polignac was imprisoned for venturing to challenge so exalted a person as the Prince of Salerno, who had insulted him. But this was not enough for the outraged Prince. One morning the Marchese, hearing a loud noise, rushed to his window to see what had happened, and was instantly shot dead by a hired bravo. The noise had been made by the Prince's orders. Elaborate duels were fought for the most absurd reasons. Thus a pet dog belonging to the Principessa di Montaguti was stolen by a maid and sold to a Spinelli, who refused to return it. He was challenged by her son, and in the duel which followed, eight combatants fought on each side. The whole party caroused together till daybreak when—*ripigliati gli sdegni*—they proceeded to the Piazza Vittoria to fight. One of them was killed, and the rest took refuge in the neighbouring churches. The other side only succeeded in wounding a Prince Pietrapasia, who retired to his villa at Posilipo. One day a boat-load of the friends of the dead man rowed to round the villa, and on his appearance opened fire on him, but failed to hit him.'[1]

In such a highly irascible age it was obviously well to take some precautions against possible reprisals of a similar nature. But Gesualdo had even more particular reasons to be on his guard against an attempt at revenge. The murdered Duke had a nephew called Fra Giulio Carafa, who, to say the least, seems to have been of a somewhat impulsive disposition. It is related of him that one

[1] *Times Literary Supplement*, 7 August 1924. Leading article, ' Naples under the Viceroys '.

day a certain poet, named Giovan Battista Arcuccio, was passing along the street, reciting his own poems as he went, in a state of lyrical exaltation, at the top of his voice. Fra Giulio Carafa, who happened to be standing at the time in front of his house, requested him to speak in a slightly more subdued tone. A few heated words ensued, after which the gentle friar, raising aloft the stick which he was carrying, smote the unfortunate poet upon the head and killed him. It is possible that the particular poem he was reciting was a very bad one, but even so the death penalty seems to us somewhat excessive. What might not Fra Giulio do under stronger provocation? One trembles in anticipation for the luckless Prince; but, as it happened, Fra Giulio, having, as we have seen, avenged the perpetration of a poem by committing a murder, proceeded now to avenge a murder by writing a poem—a sonnet in which he abused our friend the Prince in the most vehement language:

> O barbaro crudel fier omicida
> Di te stesso ministro e di vergogna,
> Il fuggir si lontan che ti bisogna?
> Forse, morto il buon Duca, ancor ti snida?
> Già non te segue Astrea, anzi ti affida
> Piu di quel che tua mente stolta agogna.
> Che temi dunque? forse ti rampogna
> Lo spirto invitto suo, forse ti sgrida?
> Esser ben puo, poi che l'offesa grave
> Fu troppo, mentre avea nudo il suo petto:
> Con molt' armi troncasti il suo bel stame.
> Qual ragion vuol che le tue macchie lave
> Sangue sparso per man di gente infame
> Se errasti tu, che mal guardasti il letto?[1]

[1] ' O barbarous, cruel and savage murderer, to your own self minister of shame, what need have you to fly away so far? Although the good Duke is dead, still thou fleest? Already Astrea ceases to pursue you, and even grants you more than your foolish mind desires. What then is it that you fear? Perchance his unconquered spirit causes you remorse, perchance reviles you. It might well be so, since the offence was too grave; seeing that when he was defenceless, with many weapons you severed the thread of his life. How could you think that blood poured out by the hands of vile creatures could wash out your dishonour while you were straying, and caring so little to keep your couch inviolate? '

Altogether the affair caused the shedding of a great deal of innocent verse. All the poets of Naples, from the great Tasso down to the obscurest rhymester of the age, seem to have burst out into a simultaneous howl of anguish over the fate of the two unfortunate lovers. A large number of these lamentations have been preserved, and though not always, or even generally, of high poetic value, they nevertheless possess a certain interest for us. In all of them, without a single exception, the sympathies are entirely on the side of the lovers; even Tasso, whose close friendship with Gesualdo, one would have thought, might have inclined him to take a different view, mourns the sad fate of the two unhappy lovers without seeming to reprove their conduct. But this is only in accordance with the spirit of the time, which regarded with a complaisance bordering almost on tacit approval, the infidelity of wives. This point of view is perhaps best summed up in the words of Bartolomeo Gottifredo, in his treatise called *Specchio d'Amore*, where he judges ' Piene di gentilezza, di cortesia, e d'umanità una giovane, la quale ai dolci preghi d'un amante, commossa, e da' suoi martiri, pietosa divenuta, del suo fedel servire finalmente degno premio gli dona '.[1] There is hardly even a suggestion of justification for Gesualdo's act; ' impious assassin ' is the politest thing said about him. All the sympathies are for Mars and Venus, none for the outraged Vulcan.

There is, however, one poem worth reproducing here, not for its poetic merits, which are slight, but because it sheds a certain light on Gesualdo's character. This is a sonnet by one Scipione Teodoro:

> Tosto che l'armi e l'omicida ha scorto
> Del consorte crudel che occide e fiede
> La bella donna, che l'amante vede
> Dest'in un punto, et assalito, e morto;
> —Ahi, crudo—disse—tu spregiasti a torto
> Le mie bellezze, e chi con ferma fede
> Amolle, uccidi, ond' or poca mercede
> Viver me fia, se la mia vita hai morto.

---

[1] ' abounding in kindness, courtesy, and humanity is the young woman who, moved by the soft entreaties of her lover and taking pity upon his torments, finally bestows upon him the worthy recompense of his devotion '.

Qui tace e mort'attende; odio e dispetto
Vincon pieta; se rende ella al furore
Del ferro e del morir mostra diletto.
Sol con la bella man ricopre il core,
Quasi spregi la vita e pregi il petto,
Ove col caro amante alberga amore.[1]

—the suggestion being that Gesualdo, after a few years of married life, had ceased to care for his wife, and had neglected her. And this may very well be true, in view of what we already know of his temperament and inclinations. What then could be more natural than that the young and beautiful Donna Maria should turn to someone who was better able to appreciate her charms?

The Duke of Andria's infatuation for her can equally well be explained. His wife, we are told, was excessively religious, and ' porto troppo nelle feste l'austerita della vita devota '. When she retired to a nunnery after her husband's death she had to be given a cell apart from the rest, because ' aveva l'anima cosi infiammata, che gliene ridondava l'ardore anche nel corpo—e le grida e i sospiri che dava fuori eran si gagliardi, da turbar la quiete e il sonno delle altre '.[2] Little wonder, then, if the Duke should prefer to sleep elsewhere than in the marital couch.

But we have not yet reached the end of this unhappy story. It is recorded that, on his arrival at Gesualdo, the Prince's fury and resentment had not yet wholly spent themselves. It seems that, in addition to the son Emmanuele, who had been left behind in Naples, Donna Maria had presented him with another child, who was then only a few months old. Believing that he recognized in its features a resemblance to the Duke of Andria, he had the cradle, and within it the unfortunate child, suspended by means of silk

---

[1] ' As soon as the fair lady did perceive the murderous arms of the cruel spouse who smites and slays, and her lover assailed and dead, she spoke as follows: " Ah, cruel one, you did wrongfully despise my charms, and now you have killed him who with firm faith cherished me; whence life is now of little consequence to me, seeing that my life is dead". With this she is silent; hatred and scorn overcome pity: she yields to the fury of the steel and shows delight in death. Only with her fair hand she shields her heart, as though she scorned her life and prized the breast that harboured love and her dear loved one.'

[2] ' her soul was in such an inflamed condition, that her ardour communicated itself to her body, and the shouts and sighs which she gave forth were of such vivacity as to disturb the peace and slumber of all the others '.

ropes attached to the four corners of the ceiling in the large hall of his castle. He then commanded the cradle to be subjected to 'violent undulatory movements', until the infant, unable to draw breath, 'rendered up its innocent soul to God'.

This ferocious act seems to have appeased the Prince's wrath. In later years, overcome by remorse for his triple crime, he caused a monastery to be built at Gesualdo in expiation of it. This monastery, the Convento dei Cappuccini, still exists, and in the church attached to it there hangs a painting of surpassing interest to us, seeing that it contains a portrait of the Prince.

At the top and in the centre of the picture the Redeemer is sitting in judgement, His right hand upraised in the act of pardoning the guilty and contrite Prince who is kneeling humbly in the lower left-hand side of the painting. On his right is sitting the Blessed Virgin Mary, who, with her right hand, is pointing to the sinner for whom she is interceding. On the left hand of the Saviour stands the archangel Michael who, with the right hand, is similarly pointing to Gesualdo for whom he is imploring pardon. Slightly lower down, on the left side of the picture, is Saint Francis, with both arms and hands outstretched in an attitude of supplication for the repentant sinner; and opposite to him is Saint Domenic, likewise invoking the Divine Mercy. Below Francis is the Magdalene, the vessel of perfume at her side, who with her face turned towards Gesualdo, seems to be exhorting him to trust in the Divine mercy of Our Lord whom she indicates to Don Carlo with both hands. Similarly, opposite to her is Saint Catherine of Siena, looking up towards the Redeemer and pointing out to him the suppliant sinner. Finally, in the lower section of the painting is the Prince himself, dressed in the Spanish fashion, kneeling bareheaded, while Saint Carlo Borromeo, Archbishop of Milan—his maternal uncle, by the way—attired in his Cardinal's robes, places his right arm protectingly on his erring nephew's shoulder, with his face turned towards the Divine Redeemer in the act of presenting him. Opposite, on the right, kneels a Franciscan nun with her hands raised in a gesture of supplication, whose identity is somewhat uncertain, though she is undoubtedly intended to represent some member of the family. Catone, in his *Memoire Gesualdine*, believes it to be

Donna Eleonora d'Este, the Prince's second wife (whom he erroneously considers to be his first wife); but it is more probably Isabella, sister of Carlo Borromeo, who became a nun with the name of Sister Corona, thus explaining the crown which she wears upon her head. In the middle of the picture is a beautiful *bambino*, representing the murdered child, with two angels at his side, while below, unfortunately hidden from sight by the altar, are two souls burning in eternal flames, which are, needless to say, intended to represent Donna Maria and the Duke of Andria.

It must be admitted that the portrait of the Prince contained in this picture makes a curiously disagreeable impression. It is not necessary to know anything of his life to detect in these long, narrow, slanting eyes with their delicate but strongly marked eyebrows, in the small, puckered, and sensual mouth, aquiline nose, and slightly receding forehead and chin, a character of the utmost perversity, cruelty and vindictiveness. At the same time it is a weak rather than a strong face—almost feminine, in fact. Physically he is the very type of the degenerate descendant of a long aristocratic line.

It is not known how long Carlo remained at Gesualdo, but in 1591 his father died, and he consequently became Prince of Venosa. Some reconciliation with the relatives of the murdered couple must, however, have been effected, for Tasso wrote to him at Naples a letter dated 19 April 1592. From this time onwards, Gesualdo's life is essentially one of intense preoccupation with music. True, he married again, as I have said, Donna Eleonora d'Este, in 1594, but this was done probably more for dynastic considerations than from inclination—like his first marriage, in fact.

However that may be, we next hear of Gesualdo at the Court of the Estes, his second wife's family, at Ferrara, in 1594. At that time Ferrara was the most cultured, enlightened, and splendid city in the whole of Italy. Indeed, one might say that Ferrara dominated the closing period of the Renaissance in Italy, as Florence dominated its early stages; the Medici were the wet nurses, the Estensi were the undertakers. With Ferrara are associated the last great writers of the Renaissance—Ariosto, Tasso, Guarini, and others of less importance individually, but nevertheless forming a

N

brilliant constellation, such as Alberto Tollio, Cinthio, Patricio, Salviati, and Pigna.

Life at the court of the last Duke, Alfonso II, was as near an approach to paradise as is permitted to mere mortals. Describing it, Annibale Romei says in the *Discorsi*: ' It was more like a royal court than that of a grand duke; for not only was it full of noble lords and valorous cavaliers, but it was also a meeting-place of the most learned and cultured spirits, and of men pre-eminent in every calling. This Prince (Alfonso II), truly admirable in all his acts, so skilfully blended business with pleasure, and so carefully apportioned both, that he did not allow himself to be wearied either by too many serious occupations or by too great a surfeit of diversions. Consequently his Grace has arranged all things in their proper season, such as, at the time of Carnival, masks, joustings, feasts, comedies, concerts, and other similar recreations, which are enjoyed in such peace and harmony that it is indeed a joy and a marvel to observe on such occasions the happiness of our city.'

And so the pleasure-loving and perhaps slightly effeminate Ferrarese, in such striking contrast to the energetic and virile Florentines, were content to remain aloof from the ceaseless turmoil and intrigue of contemporary politics, and to pass the last fleeting and irretrievable moments of the Renaissance in the splendid gardens of the Belvidere, with its groves of cypresses and plane-trees, its cool grottoes, rose gardens, and marble pavilions with their frescoed walls, among the orange and olive trees and vineyards, the air heavy with the mingled fragrance of jasmine and orange blossom: or by the side of artificial lakes whose fish had learnt to glide close to the surface of the water at the sound of a small silver bell; listening for hours on end to the stately and harmonious discourse of scholars, philosophers, and poets, and to the endless discussions so dear to the Renaissance mind, concerning beauty, truth, virtue, nobility, and so forth; and in the summer heats they would retire into *villeggiatura* at Comacchio or to the forests of Mesola where the Duke, like the fabulous Kubla Khan, had built a vast palace surrounded by twelve miles of walls enclosing numerous hunting lodges, deer parks, and marble pavilions. There they would spend the long days in hunting the wild boar, or in the chase with falcons or with hounds, and in every form of amusement which human ingenuity could devise, or the heart of man desire.

But more especially was Ferrara a city of music, the art which above all others had always been assiduously cultivated there, and in the exercise of which Ferrara had always excelled all the other cities of Italy. In the palace of the Grand Duke, according to the testimony of Ercole Bottringari, there were concerts several times every day, sometimes performed by as many as fifty-seven singers —an unprecedented number in those days. Instruments were kept constantly in tune by musicians specially maintained for the purpose, so that they could be taken up and played at a moment's notice. Instruments were made there, and the musical library was reputed to be the most extensive in the world, both in printed books and in manuscripts. And just as the Medici were themselves poets and scholars, so the princes of the Casa d'Este did not merely content themselves with favouring, protecting, and maintaining musicians at their own expense, but also practised the art themselves. From records of the times we learn that they were in the habit of procuring the most eminent professors of music available for the instruction of their children; even the pages and gentlemen-in-waiting received musical instruction, and it was rare indeed to find a gentleman at their court who was not at the same time a cultured musician.

This musical education and culture was by no means confined to the male sex. ' *Rarissime furon le donne che non cantassero o suonassero* ', and Lucrezia d'Este, afterwards Duchess of Urbino, was a veritable melomaniac. Even the nunneries were musical centres; in addition to their devotional duties, all the nuns cultivated music assiduously and frequently gave musical *soirèès* which were often attended by the whole court. Some of them even composed. One, Olimpia Leoni, was celebrated for her exquisite contralto voice and her viol playing; another, Raffaella Aleotti, for her extemporizations upon the organ and her compositions, many of which were published. Even Benvenuto Cellini, who cordially detested music, could not refrain from praising the music and musicians of Ferrara.

Moreover, all the most eminent composers of the day, and of

earlier days, were connected, directly or indirectly, with Ferrara. Brumel was *maestro di cappella* there; so was the great Josquin Desprès, who wrote there one of his most celebrated works, called after Duke Ercole II, the *Missa Hercules Dux Ferrariae*; so likewise were Vicentino, Cipriano de Rore, Luzzasco Luzzaschi,[1] and the brothers Alfonso and Francesco della Viola, all of whom spent the greater part of their active careers at Ferrara. Willaert, the maestro of San Marco in Venice, had close relations with the Estensi, to whom he presented many of his compositions. Orlando di Lasso visited Ferrara twice, in 1567 and in 1585; Luca Marenzio was *maestro di cappella* to the Cardinal Ippolito d'Este; so likewise was Palestrina himself, who also passed several years at Ferrara, and John Dowland visited the court some time between 1585 and 1595.

It is, moreover, a highly significant fact that the poets who, more than any others, were associated with the great vogue and popularity of the madrigal (the form most cultivated by musicians of the time apart from Church music)—namely, Tasso and Guarini—were all their lives intimately connected with the court of Ferrara. Another and even more important association concerns the introduction of solo singing, an innovation ascribed in all musical histories to Vincenzo Galilei, who made a setting of the Ugolino scene from Dante's *Inferno* with accompaniment of a viol about 1585, though there is evidence to show that the experiment was made, at least ten years earlier, at Ferrara, by one Vincenzo Giustiniani. When we also take into account the fact that the school of Ferrara was the one most closely identified with daring harmonic experiments, it will readily be seen that when the history of music comes to be rewritten—and the sooner it is the better— it will be found that the Ferrarese played an infinitely greater part in the idiomatic evolution of modern music than the little group of literary *dilettanti* and musical amateurs who frequented the house of Count Bardi in Florence, in the last years of the sixteenth century. In any case, the works of Peri and Caccini are devoid of

[1] Luzzaschi was a pupil of Cipriano da Rore and the master of Frescobaldi. He knew Gesualdo and dedicated his fifth book of madrigals to him (1594). For particulars of Luzzaschi's remarkable madrigals for a solo voice with instrumental accompaniment, see O. Kinkeldey, *Sammelb. d. int. Musik-Gesell*, IX.

any intrinsic musical interest, and are only historically important, which cannot be said of those of the madrigalists at the court of Ferrara.

It was, then, to this musicians' paradise that the Prince of Venosa bent his steps. According to a contemporary local scribe (*Cronaca di M. Equicola, Civica di Ferrara*), 'the Prince of Venosa, by name Carlo Gesualdo, arrived in Ferrara on the 19 February 1594 in order to wed the most illustrious Lady Donna Leonora d'Este, and took up residence at the Court with a retinue of about one hundred and fifty persons. The wedding took place on the 21st in the Estensian palace, in the chamber of our Most Serene Duchess with the Most Reverent Bishop of Ferrara officiating.

'On the 20th His Serene Highness the Duke gave a banquet for a hundred noble gentlewomen together with a few noble gentlemen. There were twenty-three courses, and ten small tables were laid out together with a large one for the Duke and the most eminent ladies, to whom were added the bride and bridegroom. After the banquet the Duke arranged a display of jousting, in which twenty-one knights on horseback and another thirty-nine on foot took part, with magnificent crested helmets and rare weapons.

'On the night of the 21st His Highness had a ballet performed in the great hall, with beautiful music, by twelve noble gentlewomen, and six of these ladies were dressed in costumes which, though made of pasteboard, had the appearance of brightly burnished metal.

'On the 22nd the Lord Don Cesare d'Este gave a sumptuous banquet at which were present the Duke and Duchess, the bride and bridegroom, and the principal nobility of the city. The table was arranged in the form of a T.'

There exists, also, I understand, though I have not seen it, a volume of verse published in celebration of the auspicious event, entitled: 'Rime di Diversi Autori nelle felicissime nozze dell' illustrissimo et eccellentissimo Signore Don Carlo Gesualdo con l'illustrissima et eccellentissima Signora Donna Leonora d'Este, Principi di Venosa. Raccolte da Don Santo Pasti, Theologo et Prete Ferrarese, e da lui a detti Signori dedicato. In Ferrara Appresso Vittorio Baldini Stampator Ducale MDXCIIII.'

He must have found the life and atmosphere in Ferrara highly congenial, for he rented the spacious palace of Marco Pio, in the Strada degli Angeli, and settled down there. He intervened with the Duke on behalf of his friend and protégé Tasso, who, though he had formerly disgraced himself by his insane exploits and behaviour at the court, desired to be forgiven and received back once more. The request, however, was not acceded to; in any case it would probably have been too late, for the unhappy poet died in 1595. Duke Alfonso II died two years later without leaving any heirs, and the city passed into the hands of the Popes. With him died the Italian Renaissance; the sunset or after-glow which had shed such a dazzling radiance died out, giving place to the all-pervading twilight of the Catholic Revival, or Counter-Reformation. All the former glory of the city departed, never to return; the palaces were deserted and gradually crumbled away into ruins, and the Belvedere gardens became a desolate wilderness—the ' *deserta bellezza di Ferrara* ' of which a later poet, Gabriele d'Annunzio, sings. All the courtiers departed. Only Marfisa d'Este remained, the lovely maenad of whom Tasso had sung when she led the revels with flushed cheeks and unbound golden hair, now grown old and grey, her thoughts occupied only with religion.

Gesualdo probably lingered on for some years after the death of the Duke; he seems then to have returned to Naples or to Gesualdo. His closing years appear to have been unhappy, if we are to trust the evidence of a chronicle entitled *Rovine di Case Napolitane del suo tempo*, by one Don Ferrante della Marra (Duca della Guardia nell' anno 1632).

' The Prince Don Carlo Gesualdo lived to see his crimes punished by God through the infliction of four great misfortunes, resulting in the total extermination of his house and race.

' The first of these was that he did suffer great shame for the space of two years, owing to the conduct of Donna Maria d'Avalos, his wife, in lying with Don Fabrizio Carafa, the Duke of Andria, almost every night, practically within sight of her husband.

' Having slain Donna Maria, by whom he had a son Don Emmanuele, Don Carlo became frenzied (*si pose Don Carlo a freneticare*) and began to treat his vassals not only avariciously and lasciviously, but also tyrannically; and owing to this, the anger of God being aroused against him, he lost a beautiful male child whom he had by Donna Eleonora d'Este, sister of the Duke of Modena, who was his first wife ' (the usual error—Donna Eleonora was his second wife), ' and this was his second great affliction.

' The third misfortune was that through the agency of God, he was assailed and afflicted by a vast horde of demons which gave him no peace for many days on end unless ten or twelve young men, whom he kept specially for the purpose, were to beat him violently three times a day, during which operation he was wont to smile joyfully. And in this state did he die miserably at Gesualdo, but not until he had lived to witness, for his fourth affliction, the death of his only son Don Emmanuele, who hated his father and had longed for his death, and, what was worse, this son died without leaving any children save only two daughters whom he had by Donna Polisena of Fustemberg (Fürstenburg?), a German princess.[1]

' And although he had arranged that the elder of these should marry within the family, his house suffered two more misfortunes. Firstly, against his express dispositions the young Princess of Venosa was married, by order of the King, to Prince Nicolino Ludovisio, nephew of the Pope, Gregory XV; and to this day she doth live at Bologna, having caused the loss to her family of the principality of Venosa, and also the estate of Gesualdo which had been in the family for little less than six hundred years.

' The second of these two other misfortunes—and to my thinking, greater than all the others—was that after the death of Don Emmanuele, the Princess Polisena went to live with her aunt, the second wife of the Prince of Caserta, Andrea Matteo Acquaviva; and having lived thus for many years did acquire an evil reputation, for not only was she all this time concubine to the said Prince, but had secretly had several children by him.

' Thus did it please God to destroy, both in possessions and in honour, a princely house which was descended from the ancient Norman kings.'

[1] Concerning Don Emmanuele, we are told that he was a poet and greatly interested in astrology (*Borzelli—Maria d'Avalos*, p. 96).

This is indeed a gloomy picture, and in spite of its undoubted exaggerations, conveys nevertheless a strong impression of authenticity. I have taken the trouble to verify the facts concerning the extinction of the House of Gesualdo, and have found the narrative strictly accurate in its details. Even the more fantastic statements, such as that concerning the horde of demons, receive striking and unexpected confirmation from a reference to Gesualdo which is to be found in a work of Thomas Campanella ' *Medicinalium juxta propria principia* '. The writer, in attributing to flagellation the virtue of curing intestinal obstructions, adduces in proof of his assertion the case of Gesualdo: ' Princeps Venusiae musica clarissimus nostro tempore cacare non poterat, nisi verberatus a servo ad id adscito.'[1]

In other words, what Ferrante della Marra calls demons, we to-day would call auto-intoxication; it is simply a matter of terminology. And, after all, does not modern medical science regard this unfortunate complaint with as much fear and superstition as our predecessors regarded demons? Is it not, in fact, believed to be the source of all the ills to which mortal flesh is subject—the Evil One himself?

Dr. Ferdinand Keiner, in his excellent little brochure *Die Madrigale Gesualdos von Venosa*, suggests that the prevailing melancholy of Gesualdo's music might be attributed to the tragic circumstances of his married life. It seems, however, much more likely that it was caused by the distressing and almost universal complaint from which he suffered. Burton, in his great work, the *Anatomy of Melancholy* (Part I, sect. 2, memb. 2, subs. 4), declares ' that costiveness and keeping in of our ordinary excrements is a cause of many diseases, and of melancholy in particular ', and supports his assertion with many concrete examples and expert medical opinions.

Carlo Gesualdo seems to have died in 1613 (not 1614 as Keiner and others say), for there is in existence a will made by him, dated

---

[1] ' The Prince of Venosa, one of the best musicians of his age, was unable to go to the stool, without having been previously flogged by a valet kept expressly for the purpose.' Thomas Campanella, *Medicinalium juxta propria*, Libri tertii, cap. III, Art. XII: ' Montrosa cura '.

3 September 1613, and opened by his wife, Donna Eleonora, on the 29th of the same month and year. Unfortunately I have not been able to obtain a copy of this interesting document. Modestino, in his book *Della Dimora di Torquato Tasso in Napoli* (Naples, 1863), quotes from it, saying that he made a copy from the original in the State Archives, which so far I have been unable to trace.

In it, Modestino tells us, the Prince invokes the intercession on his behalf of the saints represented in the picture above described. He left 40,000 ducats yearly to his widow for as long as she remained unmarried and continued to reside within the kingdom of Naples. If she did not wish to live in Gesualdo, she was given the choice of the castle at Taurasi or the palace at Naples on the shore between Mergellina and Posilippo. We learn also that he had a natural son, Don Antonio Gesualdo, to whom he left fifty ducats monthly for the duration of his life.

This will contradicts the statement of another writer, Litta, in his *Famiglie Celebri d'Italia*, where we are told that Donna Eleonora did not live long in harmony with the Prince, her husband. Complaining principally of his extreme prodigality, she petitioned the Pope for a divorce and obtained it, after which she retired to Modena, and entered the convent of Santa Eufemia, where she died in 1637. This is obviously wrong, however.

Gesualdo was buried in the chapel of Saint Ignatius in the church of the Gesu Nuovo at Naples. The inscription on his tomb was as follows:

CAROLUS GESUALDUS
COMPSAE COMES, VENUSIAE PRINCEPS,
SANCTI CAROLI BORROMEI SORORE GENITUS,
CELESTI CLARIOR COGNATIONE
QUAM REGIUM SANGUINE NORTMANNORUM
SEPULCRALI DUO HAC ARA SIBI SUISQUE ERECTA
COGNATOS CINERES, CINERI FOVET SUO,
DONEC UNA SECUM ANIMENTUR AD VITAM,
SOCIETAS IESU SIBI SUPERSTET, AC POSTERA
INTEGRE PIETATIS
OCULATA SEMPER TESTIS MEMOR.

P.

Nothing of the tomb remains. After the earthquake of 1688 the Gesu Nuovo was rebuilt and in the process the sepulchre of Gesualdo disappeared.

And this is all we know concerning the life of that most singular and delectable gentleman, His Most Illustrious and Serene Highness Don Carlo, third Prince of Venosa, eighth Count of Consa, fifteenth Lord of Gesualdo, Marquis of Laino, Rotondo, and S. Stefano, Duke of Caggiano, Lord of Frigento, Acquaputida, Paterno, S. Manco, Boneto, Luceria, S. Lupolo, etc.

Pray for his soul.

1926

Index

INDEX

Colles, H. C., 62
Collier, Hon. John, 71, 72
Connolly, Cyril, 10, 25
Constable, John, 19
Constans II, Emperor of Byzantium, 157
Cordoba, Gonsalvo Fernandez de, 159
Corelli, Angelo, 134
Cornwall, Richard of, 19
Courtauld, Samuel, 53

D

Dannreuther, Edward, 85–6, 92
Dante, Alighieri, 16, 30, 118
Debussy, Claude, 4, 26, 74, 116
Delius, Frederick, 4, 55, 70, 112, 114
Dent, Prof. E. J., 78, 152
Dentice, Scipione, 161
Desprès, Josquin, 188
Diaconus, Paulus, 158
Diaghilev, Serge, 31
Diderot, Denis, 3
Dieren, Bernard van, 52
Dietrich, Otto, 65
Disraeli, Benjamin, 5
Dohnanyi, Ernst von, 91
Donizetti, Gaetano, 97, 105, 154
Dowland, John, 188
Durante, Francesco, 103
Dvořák, Anton, 91

E

Einstein, Albert, 102
Eitner, Robert, 149
Elgar, Edward, 20, 25–6, 79, 92
Eliot, T. S., 4
Epstein, Jacob, 33–4
Ercole II, Duke of Ferrara, 188
Este, Alfonso II, Duke d', 186, 190
Este, Don Cesare d', 189
Este, Donna Eleonora d', 185, 189, 191
Este, Cardinal Ippolito D', 188
Este, Lucrezia d', 187
Este, Marfisa d', 190
Eumorfopoulos, M., 53
Eybler, Joseph, 123

F

Fétis, Francois, 95, 98–9
Filomarino, Fabrizio, 161
Flaubert, Gustave, 69, 110
France, Anatole, 69, 178
Francis, Saint, 82
Franck, César, 91
Fustemberg, Donna Polisena of, 191
Fux, Johann, 132

196

G

Gabrieli, Giovanni, 148
Galilei, Vincenzo, 188
Gallup (Survey), 22
Garbo, Greta, 37
Gardano, Antonio, 148
Garibaldi, Giuseppe, 4
Gauguin, Paul, 70, 112
Gautier, Theophile, 49
GESUALDO, Carlo, vii, 157 et seq.
Gesualdo, Cardinal Alfonso, 159
Gesualdo, Don Antonio, 193
Gesualdo, Ascanio, 159
Gesualdo, Don Emmanuele, 163, 183, 190
Gesualdo, Elia, 158
Gesualdo, Fabrizio, 159
Gesualdo, Don Giulio, 165
Gesualdo, Guglielmo, 158
Gesualdo, Isabella, 160
Gesualdo, Luigi, 159, 162
Gesualdo, Niccolo, 158
Gesualdo, Ruggiero, 159
Gesualdo, Lady Sveva, 171
Gesualdo, Vittoria, 160
Giuliano, Don Alfonso di, 163
Giustinani, Vincenzo, 188
Glazounov, Alexander, 91, 129
Gluck, Christoph von, 70, 144
Goebbels, Joseph, 5
Goethe, J. W. von, 30, 63, 144
Gogh, Vincent van, 112
Goldmark, Karl, 67
Gottifredo, Bartolomeo, 182
Gourdjieff, Ivan, 38
Graves, Robert, 24, 26
Gregory XV, Pope, 191
Grieg, Edvard, 91
Grifone, Antonio, 161
Grouchy, General, 5
Grove, Sir George, 95–6, 100, 132, 152
Guarini, Battista, 185, 188
Gubbins, Nathaniel, 6
Guiscard, Robert, 158

H

Handel, Frederick, 130, 132, 144
Handke, R., 128, 129
Hauptmann, Moritz, 95
Haydn, Joseph, 114
Hegel, G. W. F., 3, 14
Heine, Heinrich, 89, 144
Herder, Johann Gottfried, 61
Heseltine, Philip, vii
Hiller, J. A., 130
Hindemith, Paul, 45
Hitler, Adolf, 5

PRINTED IN GREAT BRITAIN AT
THE BOWERING PRESS, PLYMOUTH